BINDING THE STRONGMAN

BISHOP ABRAHAM
CHIGBUNDU

This Book is a Gift

____

From

____

To

____

On the Occasion of

____

Date

BINDING THE STRONG MAN

ISBN:9789785764598

Unless otherwise indicated, all scriptural references are from the King James Version of the Holy Bible.

Please note we capitalize certain pronouns in Scripture that refer to the Father, Son, and Holy Spirit, and may differ from some Bible publisher's style. Take note also that the name satan and related names are not capitalized. We choose not to acknowledge him, even to the point of violating grammatical rules.

PUBLISHED IN UNITED STATES OF AMERICA BY:

FREEDOM PUBLICATIONS
21, Adesuwa Grammar School Road, GRA.
P.O.BOX 7240, Benin City, Nigeria.
Tel: 08022908737, 08023381077
Email: bishopchigbundu@gmail.com
Website: www.voiceoffreedomonline.com

DESIGN & PRINTS :
Aaron & Hur Publishing (*A member of the Aaron & Hur Group*)
16, Thomas Salako Street, Ogba-Ikeja **T:** 07035121346, 08097032664
Email: aaronandhurpublishing@gmail.com
Website: www.aaronandhurpublishing.com

TABLE OF CONTENTS

DEDICATION

This book is dedicated to my darling wife, Rev (Mrs.) Florence Chigbundu, my jewel of inestimable value. It is also dedicated to my lovely children, Emmanuel, Faith, Mike and David, you all remain sources of inspiration to me.

May God richly reward all of you in Jesus name. Amen.

ACKNOWLEDGEMENTS

I am deeply appreciative of all those who in one way or the other, contributed towards the success of the publication of this book.

I wish to thank my daughter, Pastor Anthonia Innocent for her great inputs in editing this work. God richly bless you.

Special appreciation to Basola Victor and his creative team at Aaron & Hur Publishing, Lagos for their professionalism and dedication in the production of this book.

INTRODUCTION

Life is not a fun fare. Life is a warfare; and if you refuse to engage in warfare, your life can never fare well. Whether you look for trouble or not, the day you crossed from darkness to light, you have already entered into a battle with the kingdom of darkness.

This is not just a general battle, but a specific battle with the strong man assigned against your life from the pit of hell. Ignorance or denial of the existence of the strongman is not an excuse neither is it an opportunity to escape its onslaught.

The enemy you do not know, you cannot kill. You have suffered enough, it's time to identify, unmask, and deal with him once and for all.

In this book, you will discover who the strongman is,

the different types of strongmen and their characteristic features and also how to deal with them.

Do yourself a favour, do not only buy this book, read it and practice what you learn from it until you receive your outstanding testimony.

God bless you richly.

Bishop Dr. Abraham Chigbundu
Benin City, Nigeria
June, 2020

ONE

WHO IS THE STRONG MAN?

Chapter One

"

The spiritual realm is a very vast and complicated realm hence novices don't fight there and return same, complete or alive.

"

Chapter One

WHO IS THE STRONG MAN?

•●⬤●•

But if I cast out devils by the spirit of God, then the kingdom of God is come unto you. Or else how can one enter into a STRONG MAN'S house and spoil his goods, except he first bind the STRONG MAN? and then he will spoil his house.
Matt. 12:28-29

Life is not a fun fare. Life is a warfare; and if you refuse to engage in warfare, your life can never fare well. The reason is simply because whether you look for trouble or not, the day you crossed from darkness to light, you already entered into battle with the kingdom of darkness. Battles and enemies need no invitation; whether you are prepared for them or not, they shall surely come.

And they shall fight against thee; but they shall not prevail against thee; for I am with thee, saith the LORD, to deliver thee. Jer. 1:19

The Bible did not say they "may" fight against you. No! It says, they "shall" fight against you. This indicates that the attack is not a probable occurrence but a certainty. Warfare is part of your core course in the school of life. You don't run away from fights because in successfully contending with the enemies lies your promotion.

Until you begin to confront certain challenges in your life, you are not ready to ***take the front row in life***. The front row is for overcomers so if you are not ready for confrontation, then you are not ready to overcome. There is no major victory you will ever record in your life that you will not have to fight for.

And from the days of John the Baptist until now, the kingdom of heaven suffereth violence, and the violent taketh it by force. Matt. 11:12

When Esau returned to be blessed after Jacob had collected his birthright, he cried to his father for just one blessing and his father made certain pronouncements to him that you will do well to take to heart!

> *And by thy sword shalt thou live, and shalt serve thy brother; and it shall come to pass WHEN THOU SHALT HAVE THE DOMINION, that thou shalt break his yoke from off thy neck. Gen. 27:40*

The implication of the highlighted phrase above is that when you are no longer comfortable with your situation, when you are sick and tired of being sick and tired, when you become restless on account of the bondage or affliction, then you will fight and break the yoke of your oppressor from off your neck by yourself!

> *Shake thyself from the dust; arise, and sit down, O Jerusalem: LOOSE THYSELF from the bands of thy neck, O captive daughter of Zion. Isaiah 52:2*

Esau took his father's counsel to heart so much so that when he met his brother several years later, despite not receiving a blessing from his father, he had become so blessed that he declined the gifts from Jacob because he didn't need them. By his refusal, he was in effect saying to his younger brother who had denied him the blessing many years ago, "I too, have made it; I have enough"! Glory to God in the highest!

> *And he said, What meanest thou by all this drove which I met? And he said, These are to find grace in the sight of my lord. And Esau said, I HAVE ENOUGH, my brother; KEEP THAT THOU HAST UNTO THYSELF. Gen. 33:8-9*

Spiritual warfare is war in the spirit realm between humans and spirits and also between humans and human agents of darkness who are possessed and engaged by evil spirits to carry out dark and sinister assignments. In this war, only spiritual weapons and spiritual powers are used. All physical weapons are useless.

> *For though we walk in the flesh, we do not WAR after the flesh: For the weapons of our warfare are not carnal but mighty through God to the pulling down of strongholds; 2 Cor. 10:3-4*

Child of God, you are in a warfare and the sooner you come to terms with this, the better for you. A general in the army can be harassed by kindergarten witches in the night if he lacks spiritual powers.

We become involved in some unnecessary (avoidable) spiritual warfare when we neglect to engage the necessary spiritual warfare to ward off the unnecessary ones. We have mighty weapons to pull down and demolish the strongholds of the strongman but we will not be able to access our goods if we don't make use of those weapons.

The spiritual realm is a vast and complicated realm hence novices don't fight there and return same, complete or alive.

The battle against the strongman is one of the major battles you must fight and conquer on time otherwise you may not be able to maximize your potentials in this life.

> *But if I cast out devils by the spirit of God, then the kingdom of God is come unto you. Or else how can one enter into a STRONG MAN'S house and spoil his goods, except he first bind the STRONG MAN? And then he will spoil his house.*
> *Matt. 12:28-29*

I say this because the word BIND does not sound to me like a peaceful word, and no strong man will willingly or peacefully offer you his hands to bind without a fight. There is nowhere on earth that slaves receive their freedom peacefully, it is usually forcefully demanded for or wrestled out.

In the above scriptures, Jesus made us to understand that there is an armed strong man whose assignment is to capture goods and keep them in his palace. He said the goods in the strong man's custody will remain secure until one stronger than him comes, overpowers and disarms him before the goods can be recovered.

If Jesus recognized that there is a strong man, and Apostle Paul buttressed this by speaking of strong holds, principalities, powers, rulers and spiritual wickedness in heavenly places that confront us on daily basis, then you better believe it that we have a lot of work – spiritual warfare, to engage in.

> *For though we walk in the flesh, we do not war after the flesh: For the weapons of our warfare are not carnal but mighty through God to the pulling down of strongholds; Casting down every high thing that exalteth itself against the knowledge of God, and bringing into captivity every thought to the obedience of Christ.* 2 Cor. 10:3-5

Beloved, I want you to understand that **there can be no stronghold without a strong man and there can't be a stronghold if there is no treasure to be captured.**

It is useless dealing with the stronghold without first dealing with the strong man. If you deal with the stronghold without dealing with the strong man, he will simply build another stronghold.

Interestingly, when the strong man has occupied a place for so long, it gives him the effrontery to even call the place his house. You know, when a tenant has lived in a compound for so long, if you don't make necessary enquiries, he may begin to fancy himself as the landlord, and go on to assume that role. The strong man has the boldness to call the place his house because over the years, the owner has not gotten up to confront and contend with him.

> *When the unclean spirit is gone out of a man, he walketh through dry places, seeking rest; and finding none, he saith, I WILL RETURN UNTO MY HOUSE whence I came out. Luke 11:24*

What audacity! The analogy that comes to mind here is that of an uncompleted building taken over by the destitute and street urchins unhindered for years. They will continue to reside there free of charge and some unscrupulous elements amongst the free dwellers may even begin to lay claim to the property if the owners don't show up to assert authority.

In fact, amongst land grabbers, I came to find out that there are some wicked charms used against land owners that make them forget their lands as long as they live unless God intervenes. And if you don't know or remember what belongs to you, how then can you place a demand for it?

The battle against the strong man is a battle that the devil does not joke with because he knows that if you succeed in defeating him, you will not only fulfill destiny but also every other battle in your life will be a walk over. The moment David killed Goliath, every other Philistine soldier lost the morale to fight and they all suffered a similar fate as their champion!

It is mandatory for us as citizens of heaven, to understand these powers and destroy them so as to have our destinies manifest in its due season. In Psalm 90:12, the Bible clearly indicates that our time on earth is limited, when the Psalmist prayed, "*So teach us to number our days, that we may apply our hearts to wisdom.*" We must therefore apply wisdom to maximize the opportunities allocated to us within the various seasons of our lives. The assignment of the strong man is to map out various strategies to waste our seasons so we don't become what we were created to be.

If he knows that he may not be able to utterly deny you your destiny, he vigorously fights so it may be delayed in which case, you will have only limited time to manifest.

Friend, there is a strong man in every life, family, village, community and city. There is a strong man assigned over every marriage, finance, business, company, profession, health, government and various systems in life.

Things don't just happen. There are forces that manipulate the affairs of men on earth and those forces are called strong men.

In 2Corinthians 10:3-6, Paul says: *"Though we walk in the flesh, we do not war after the flesh..."*

In other words, although we live in the physical world, and experience our challenges here, what confronts us is sponsored from the spiritual realm. The physical realm resembles the spiritual but it is the spiritual realm that controls the physical.

Before I go further, I want you to know that as children of the most High God, we are not in any way taking a defensive posture in this battle. Christians are already assured of victory as we contend with the strong man.

Rise ye up, take your journey, and pass

over the river Arnon: behold, I HAVE GIVEN INTO THINE HAND SIHON THE AMORITE, king of Heshbon, and his land: BEGIN TO POSSESS IT, AND CONTEND WITH HIM IN BATTLE. Deut. 2:24

WHO IS THE STRONG MAN?

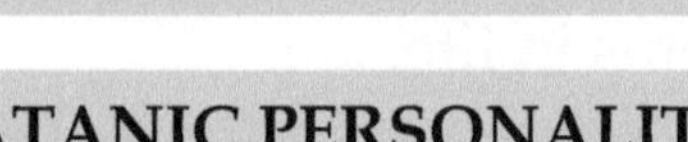

HE IS A SATANIC PERSONALITY IN CHARGE OF OR RESPONSIBLE FOR A STRONGHOLD.

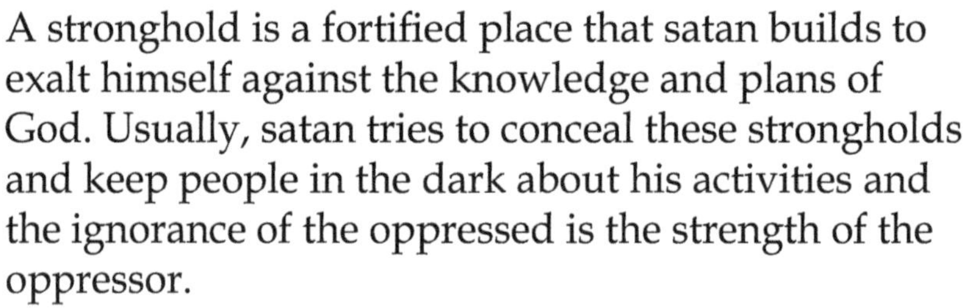

A stronghold is a fortified place that satan builds to exalt himself against the knowledge and plans of God. Usually, satan tries to conceal these strongholds and keep people in the dark about his activities and the ignorance of the oppressed is the strength of the oppressor.

The worst thing that can happen to any man is to be in bondage and not be aware of it. Satan always tries to operate under the cover of darkness and the only thing that exposes him is the light of God's Word. The illumination that comes from the Word of God is what exposes satanic strongholds and by extension, the strong man.

When satan's stronghold remains concealed and shrouded in mystery, the strong man is safe and can operate without being identified. But as soon as he is exposed, the battle is half won and that is why identifying the strong man is of absolute importance.

A STRONG MAN IS SATAN'S DELEGATED AUTHORITY OVER A STRONGHOLD.

He may have other servant spirits operating under his domain of authority to make the victim's life worse, but the strong man is the ruler spirit. That is why dealing with one of the sub spirits does not solve the problems, you need to identify and bind the strong man.

When Jesus encountered the mad man of Gaderene, He didn't address the other servant spirits who had also invaded the man's life, he went straight for the ruler spirit. Jesus knew that if he focused on the strong man, it would save him time, effort and energy.

> *For he said unto HIM, Come out of the man, THOU unclean spirit. And he asked HIM, What is THY name? And HE answered, saying, my name is Legion: for we are many. And he besought him much that he would not send them away out of the country. Now there was there nigh unto the mountains a great herd of swine*

feeding. And all the devils besought him, saying, Send us into the swine, that we may enter into them. And forthwith Jesus gave them leave. And the unclean spirits went out, and entered into the swine: and the herd ran violently down a steep place into the sea, (they were about two thousand;) and were choked in the sea. Mark 5:8-13

Jesus identified the strong man and dealt with him in the first person. And when He did, He was able to set the man free of the other demons irrespective of their number.

A STRONG MAN IS THE POWER THAT RULES AND LIMITS THE PROGRESS OF A PARTICULAR FAMILY.

If you look carefully into some families you will observe that all the members are not able to succeed beyond a particular level, no matter their field of endeavor. This is because the strong man frustrates every effort they make to succeed beyond where he has pegged their success or progress. Any member of such a family who in the flesh, persists in their attempts to exceed the satanic limit is usually visited with one tragedy or another.

HE IS THE RULER SPIRIT THAT HINDERS THE PROGRESS OF SONS AND DAUGHTERS OF A PARTICULAR VILLAGE.

This is why some villages experience a lot of backwardness because their sons and daughters at home or abroad also experience limitations. It is a well-known fact that distance is not a barrier in the spirit realm. Due to the activities of this strong man in such villages, even government developments characteristically pass them by.

THE STRONG MAN IS THE MANAGING DIRECTOR OF SATANIC WAREHOUSES WHERE THE BLESSINGS OF A PERSON, A PARTICULAR FAMILY OR VILLAGE ARE CAGED.

As it is in the physical, so it is in the spirit realm and vice versa. When thieves rob a person or place, the stolen goods are kept in a safe place till they can be safely disposed of. Like I said before, a stronghold is a satanic warehouse where peoples' stolen blessings or treasures are kept safe by satan, and the strong man is the power that employs all manner of evil strategies to ensure stolen treasures kept in such warehouses remain intact, far from the reach of the rightful owners.

HE IS THE DOMINATING INFLUENCE OVER YOUR PRESENT NEGATIVE SITUATION.

He is the reason some people suffer certain disadvantages even though they are surrounded by the means to change, improve or totally heal their situation or circumstance. The strong man denies them access to whatever way of escape whether financial, spiritual, human or material which God has made available to them.

HE IS THE EVIL MONITORING SPIRIT ASSIGNED TO MONITOR EVERY STEP YOU TAKE TOWARDS PROGRESS.

And that is why it looks as if your problem intensifies any time you take a step towards solution because the strong man monitors you to ensure you don't break free.

THE STRONGMAN IS THE SPIRIT THAT PROLONGS YOUR SUFFERING, TEARS AND HARDSHIP.

In life, we will all go through challenges; no one is immune to them. However, when difficulties persist and / or move from one level of complication to another, then the strong man is on active duty there.

He thrives on people's pains so he works to keep people miserable and unfulfilled by perpetuating their negative experiences.

HE IS THE SPIRIT THAT DECREASES YOUR INCOME WHILE MULTIPLYING YOUR EXPENDITURE.

He stirs up money draining problems round about you and at the same time, denies you the means to solve the problems. Some people lose their jobs or make a huge business loss then just as they are trying to come to terms with that, a loved one takes ill, or their only vehicle breaks down or that is the time robbers remember to visit their home, etc.

HE IS THE SPIRIT THAT FRUSTRATES ANYTHING THAT WILL ENHANCE YOUR FUTURE.

The strong man works to steal, kill or destroy anything that will enhance your glorious future. If it is a relationship that will eventually prosper you, he causes a strain or actual disconnection, if it is a project or transaction, unforeseen complications suddenly arise just to stall or terminate the venture.

HE ENSURES YOUR SEED DIES IN THE GROUND.

The seeds referred to here could be financial or

human. His assignment is to kill your seeds, however healthy they may be, and indeed, what is the benefit of a seed that refuses to germinate? If he cannot out rightly kill the seeds, he ensures their growth is stunted and that they yield any reasonable fruit that will justify all the labour bestowed. At the end of the day, the victim's expectation is denied them.

HE MANIPULATES YOUR MIND TO MAKE WRONG CHOICES.

This is the reason some people prefer to enjoy present pleasure to the detriment of their future treasure, then in the future they will live under pressure that would have easily been avoided. The future is so far in the mind of these ones and the enemy keeps them occupied with trivialities which profit them very little or nothing. They fantasize and pay lip service to their great future but their present lifestyle points only to a future full of frustration.

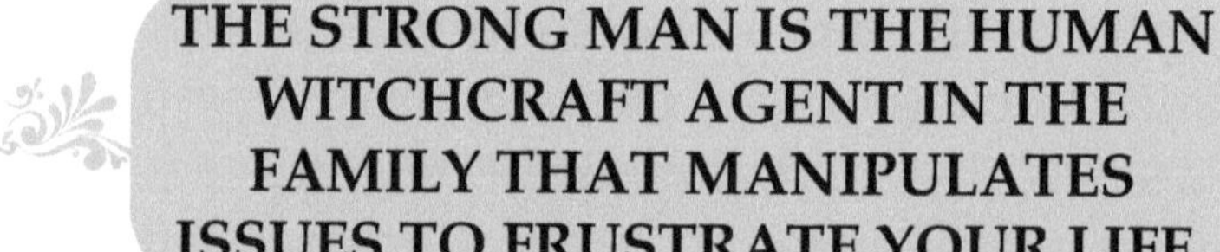

THE STRONG MAN IS THE HUMAN WITCHCRAFT AGENT IN THE FAMILY THAT MANIPULATES ISSUES TO FRUSTRATE YOUR LIFE.

These witchcraft agents are usually difficult to deal with because they are "insiders". It requires adequate knowledge of the nature and manifestations of this spirit and the anointing of God to dislodge them.

HE IS THE CONTROLLING ANCESTRAL AND FAMILY ALTAR THAT SPONSORS WITCHCRAFT TO ENFORCE THE EXISTING EVIL PATTERNS IN THE FAMILY.

HE IS THE POWER IN CHARGE OF INVISIBLE LAWS THAT MAKE THE MEMBERS OF A PARTICULAR FAMILY LAWFUL CAPTIVES.

He thrives on the ignorance of the members of the family to keep them bound. He either keeps them in the dark about the existence of spiritual laws fostering their captivity, or he makes them doubt that such laws do exist.

> *Shall the prey be taken from the mighty, or the lawful captive delivered but thus saith the LORD, even the captives of the mighty shall be taken away and the prey of the terrible shall be delivered: for I will contend with him that contendeth with thee and I will save thy children.*
> *Isaiah 49:24-26*

In *Jeremiah 22:29-30,* a decree was made on the sand (altar) against a man and his seed to the effect that they would be childless and poor, and royalty was denied them.

> *O earth, earth, earth, hear the word of the LORD, write this man childless, a man that shall not prosper in his days: for no man of his seed shall prosper, sitting upon the throne of David, and ruling anymore in Judah. Jer. 22:29-30*

By this pronouncement, a strong man was assigned to this family to accomplish these decrees and if nobody identifies and destroys it, it will run from generation to generation.

> *Give them, O LORD: what wilt thou give? Give them a miscarrying womb and dry breasts. Hosea 9:14*

In the scripture above, God was so angry with Ephraim that He promised to give them a miscarrying womb and a dry breast. What a decree against a nation as a result of their disobedience! When a womb cannot retain conception it means it cannot produce babies and this keeps the breast dry. The moment such a pronouncement goes forth, a curse is activated and a strong man is assigned to enforce it.

Three things are involved in the above pronouncement which I will use to explain manifestations of the strong man in many people's lives.

They are:
1. Barrenness
2. Miscarriage or Abortion
3. Still birth

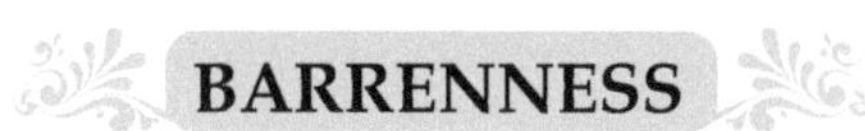

BARRENNESS

Barrenness simply means lack of or inability to maximize opportunities in life. Opportunities are tied to seasons and when you miss your season and the opportunities allocated to you, you will not manifest your destiny early or you may not even manifest at all. Barrenness is against God's original plan for man as recorded in Gen. 1:28

> *And God blessed them, and God said unto them, Be fruitful, and multiply and replenish the earth, and subdue it: and have dominion over the fish of the sea, and over the fowl of the air, and over every living thing that moveth upon the earth. Gen. 1:28*

The evidence of barrenness is a life devoid of results.

You will agree with me that your generation will not reckon with you until your evidence manifests to all.

Evidence is a direct product of maximized opportunities. **New seasons are often heralded by new opportunities.** Certain opportunities are tied to a particular season of your life; if you fail to access and maximize the opportunities within that season, it means you have lost that opportunity and wasted that season.

MISCARRIAGE OR ABORTION

This speaks of the interruption of a process to prevent the production of a product. When the spirit of abortion or miscarriage besieges a man's life, he will always start something new but never produce evidence. He will keep initiating something new but never bring it to fruition by completing it. A life suffering from this wicked spirit will be plagued with many abandoned projects. He will always be full of dreams, projects, ideas but no product. The spirit of abortion causes a man to go through a process without any visible product to show for it.

Under normal circumstances, the pain of laboring over a process is quickly forgotten once the product arrives but if you labour without any tangible product to show for it, what worthless pain!

STILL BIRTH

When this wicked spirit is sponsored by the strong man, people will see your efforts but the fruit of all the toiling will be dead on arrival. People will see you investing but the outcome will be a total loss. The victim of this foul spirit may begin a building project, in the end it will be discovered that the land was sold to him by the wrong person, so in anger; the rightful owner will pull the illegal structure down. Still birth! The victim may succeed in buying a car - only for it to be stolen few hours later. After several years of saving up income, the first consignment of goods to be imported by a victim of this terrible spirit might be seized and confiscated! There will always be one tale of woe or another waiting at the door of the victim's breakthrough.

Barrenness, Abortion and Still birth equals poverty!

TYPES OF STRONG MEN

Daniel's experience in chapter 10:12-13, reveals the activities of the strong man against our answered prayer.

> *Then said he unto me, Fear not, Daniel: for from the first day that thou didst set thine heart to understand and to chasten thyself before thy God, thy words were heard and I am come for thy words. But the prince of Persia*

withstood me one and twenty days: but lo, Michael, one of the chief princes, came to help me; and I remained there with the kings of Persia. Dan. 10:12-13

Let's now take a look at five types of strong men:

TERRITORIAL STRONG MAN

This is a strong man in charge of a particular territory, whose assignment is to hinder the progress and blessings of people within that territory. He makes sure nothing good or significant happens in that environment.

When a territorial strong man is in charge of an environment, you will notice certain negative behavioral patterns, destructive habits and prevailing evils. Why? The character of the prevailing spirit controlling an environment usually will become the character of the people in that particular environment. That is why you will notice that a particular environment will have a high rate of single mothers and unwanted pregnancies while in some others, the men are irresponsible; it is the women who feed the men, etc.

If perchance you relocate to such environment and you don't identify and deal with the strong man in that place, just get ready to suffer whatever they are suffering as much as they suffer it because sooner than later, by virtue of your residence in the vicinity under his control, your name will enter the strong man's list. Satan knows no mercy, he is no respecter of any laws of justice and your sincere ignorance of his operations will not suffice.

To identify the strong man prevalent over a particular territory, investigate the following:

1. The prevalent lifestyle of the people living there.
2. The culture, traditions and beliefs that dominate that geographical area.
3. The extent of the penetration of the gospel and persistent challenges.

ANCESTRAL STRONG MAN

This is the strong man who operates from village altars. It is the spirit that manipulates and dictates the level of success and achievements of sons and daughters from a particular village.

FAMILY STRONG MAN

This is the strong man from the altar of a particular family with the assignment to execute the details of the ancestral family covenant (s) on every member of the family.

BLOODLINE STRONG MAN

This strong man is the witchcraft spirit that ensures

that evil family patterns are transferred through the blood line. He perpetuates the observation of family rites, rituals and traditions. Below are some of the patterns in different families:

- Untimely death of family members at a particular age.
- Divorce amongst daughters or sons at a particular age of the marriage. I have seen families where divorce takes place at the birth of the third child. I once counseled a woman from a family where divorce takes place as soon they are forty years of age.
- Young widows or widowers. In the families with this pattern, the men will always lose their first wife at an early age and they will marry a second wife later. It means when you become the first wife of any of the men in this family, you have signed your death certificate.
- Late marriages. This pattern ensures that members of this family marry very late which results among others, to limited number of children.
- No marriage. In families with this pattern, they are plagued with the spirit of celibacy. They desire to get married but never do; rather they co - habit with someone, have children and move on as single parents.
- Sickness. There are many families with a pattern of different kinds of sicknesses and diseases. I have seen families whose sons or daughters go mad after marriage. In some

families, it is blindness at a particular age. I encountered a family of nine children and six of them had mental problems. Another family had three handsome sons, all deaf and dumb.

- Incomplete projects and studies. Members of this family will always start a project or building but will not finish it. They may embark on writing a book for several years but never get around to having it published. If they are in any institute of learning, their studies will always be interrupted by one occurrence or the other.
- Poverty of the first sons. In this kind of family, the pattern that runs in the blood line is that first sons don't succeed. I happen to come from a village where the destiny of the first sons was mortgaged to an ancestral deity. I was the first son, my father was the first son and his father was the first son. I did not know why I had to go through so much poverty as a pastor, until God showed me the pattern in my lineage. It wasn't until I broke the yoke before I experienced prosperity.
- Children outside marriage. I have ministered to a lot of people under this pattern. In this family or village, it is normal to have children outside wedlock or you must have a child before you can get married. In many cases, if you escape this pattern and marry, the powers will either break the marriage or make you barren. But thank God, by the power of the Holy Spirit,

many have been set free.

- Disappointment. There are families that suffer from this pattern of mysterious disappointments at the eleventh hour. They experience disappointments in marriage, business, social relationships and other areas not mentioned here. Members of this family have catalogues of disappointments in many areas of their lives. You must break this pattern now if you observe it in your family.
- Struggle and Hardship. In this family, good things never come easy. No matter their educational achievements, skills and talents, they experience strange struggles and hardship in all their endeavours. This pattern limits their achievements in life.
- Underachievement. This is a wicked pattern. The victims here are educated, have the right connections but characteristically achieve below their capacity. They have all it takes to be on top but they never get there because of the activities of this spirit.
- Losses. This is the spirit of failure. It makes you lose what you have laboured to achieve. The essence is to bring you back to zero point.

However, child of God, no matter how bad your case is, all these patterns can be destroyed in the name of Jesus. The reason many have tried to destroy them and failed is because they did not address the strong man behind the pattern.

Every pattern is a product of the pronouncements, incantations, covenants and promises made by previous generations on ancient altars. It will also interest you to know that witchcraft spirit is the executor of the covenants and dictates of the strong man in a family. Binding witchcraft spirit and breaking the pattern will not produce the desired result until you destroy the altar that empowered the strong man who established the pattern.

Take the following steps if you are really ready to terminate strange patterns from your life:

1. Identify the altar if possible or use your family name or village name.
2. Destroy the altar and the strong man behind the altar.
3. Destroy witchcraft spirits and activities.
4. Destroy the patterns.
5. Establish your own pattern.
6. Take a painful sacrifice to your man of God who will make new decrees on your life.

HIRED STRONG MAN

These are satanic human agents who are hired to afflict you with all the evil they can. They are most dangerous because they could either be related to you or live or work in the same house or office with you. They fall into the following categories: Witch doctors, Native doctors, Occult practitioners, false Prophets, Diviners, Enchanters, Alfas, etc.

Here is a list of some hired strong men as recorded in the Bible:

- Balaam. In Numbers 23:1-8, he demanded twenty-one cows and twenty-one rams to raise twenty-one altars to curse the Israelites.
- Delilah. She was Samson's woman friend yet she received a bribe of eleven thousand pieces of silver from each of the lords of the Philistines and betrayed him. (Judges 16:5)
- Judas. In Luke 22, Judas was one of Jesus' disciples and the treasurer of Jesus' ministry; yet he betrayed his Master for thirty pieces of silver.
- Haman. In Esther 3:1-15, _Haman consulted with spirits for one year to determine the exact day and month to successfully destroy the Jews. He offered ten thousand talents of silver for the execution of this conspiracy.
- Joseph's brothers. According to Genesis 37:26-28, they collected twenty pieces of silver and sold him into slavery so that his dream to rule over them will not come to pass.

The hired strong man doesn't work alone, they are connected to the following: ancestral altars, family altars, water spirit altars, witchcraft altars and occult altars.

The good news is, irrespective of the nomenclature of the strong man, the name of Jesus is higher than every other name.

TWO

BIBLICAL CHARACTERISTICS OF THE STRONGMAN

Chapter Two

"

If we must fare well in any task or project
in the natural or spiritual realm,
we must engage in spiritual warfare

"

Chapter Two

BIBLICAL CHARACTERISTICS OF THE STRONGMAN

•●⬤●•

For though we walk in the flesh, we do not war after the flesh: For the weapons of our warfare are not carnal but mighty through God to the pulling down of strongholds; Casting down every high thing that exalteth itself against the knowledge of God, and bringing into captivity every thought to the obedience of Christ. 2 Cor. 10:3-5

Every family, life and territory has a strong man empowered by the devil to carry out his wicked plans and agenda. If the Bible specifically recognizes a person or spirit as a strong man, then we have to pay attention to that person, spirit or subject if we are serious about manifesting our glorious destiny.

What or who is the strong man? For some, this question elicits the image of a huge, foreboding creature with its wings spread over a city. Others think of someone like Hitler who threatens the peace of nations and people groups.

Which is right? Is the strong man a ruler of darkness, as mentioned in Ephesians 6:12, or is he an actual person who through some dark, charismatic influence is able to control governments, laws, and the thinking pattern of people?

Ezekiel chapter 28 is one among other scriptures that helps throw more light on this matter. At the beginning of this scripture, God is evidently speaking through the prophet Ezekiel of judgment against the (human) prince of Tyre. However, from verses 12 to 19, the same king of Tyre is addressed as having supernatural attributes.

In the same passage, there appears to be a physical ruler being addressed as well as a supernatural being who stands behind the human structure. That means the strong man can be both spiritual and physical. The spiritual strong man usually has a physical representative empowered by forces of darkness to exert influence over a life, family or territory.

If we must fare well in any assignment whether in the natural or spirit realm, we must engage in spiritual warfare (Ephesians 6:12). In Mark 3:27, Jesus said, *"No one can enter a strongman's house and plunder his goods, unless he first binds the strong man. And then he will plunder his house."*

But you will agree with me that you cannot enter into the house of the enemy if you don't first identify the enemy and its specific abode because like I earlier stated, the strong man has the audacity to call the place where he resides his house. What I still don't understand is what gives him that audacity because the Bible says our bodies are temples of the Holy Spirit (1Cor. 6:19)

> *What? know ye not that your body is the temple of the Holy Ghost which is in you, which ye have of God, and ye are not your own?*

Jesus, speaking in Luke 11:24 said;

> *When the unclean spirit is gone out of a man, he walketh through dry places, seeking rest; and finding none, he saith, I will return unto my house whence I came out.*

Here, you can hear the evil spirit talking again, calling the man's body "his house". What an audacious assertion - an illegal occupant laying claims of ownership to another person's property!

But I also discovered from scriptures that when Adam and Eve sinned, they turned over the title deed of the earth to satan who is called the "god of the world" in 2 Corinthians 4:4, "prince of this world" in John 14:30 and "prince of the power of the air" in Ephesians 2:2.

In 1 John 5:19, the Apostle John said, "We know that we are of God, and that the whole world lies in the grip of the evil one."

Sin can make a man loose authority over his life, family or territory to the devil. It will interest you to know that demons understand rights and legislations and will not lay claim to a life, family or territory without legal transactions, agreements or covenants which authorize transfer of ownership.

If you go on to study the book of Isaiah chapter 49:24-25, you will discover an eye opening revelation.

> *Shall the prey be taken from the mighty, or the LAWFUL CAPTIVE delivered? But thus saith the LORD, Even the captives of the mighty shall be taken away, and the prey of the terrible shall be delivered: for I will contend with him that contendeth with thee, and I will*

save thy children. Isa. 49:24-25

Can you see that dealing with the strong man is a serious battle because the strong man has right over his territory? If Isaiah calls the victims "lawful" captives, then that means the captors are "lawful" captors who are only enforcing a lawful deed.

God's promise to deliver and also save your children is only a guarantee that you will overcome in warfare, not an exemption because if you run from the fight, your children too will partake of the bondage.

The strong man is our adversary, opposing the things of God, the church and every born again believer. He is an enemy that is fighting hard against us, unleashing his arsenals against the souls of mankind, against everyone who is seeking to do the will of God, and especially men and women of God who are doing what they can to make an impact for the kingdom of God.

Apostle Peter said, *"Your adversary, the devil, prowls around like a roaring lion, seeking someone to devour" (1 Peter 5:8)*. Paul affirmed this by saying, *"We wrestle not against flesh and blood, but against principalities, against powers, against the rulers of the darkness of this world, against spiritual wickedness in high places" (Ephesians 6:12)*.

IDENTIFYING THE STRONG MAN

You cannot confront what you have not identified. **The enemy you do not know, you cannot kill.** For you to win a battle, you must know your enemies, their strength, and mode of operation.

Many Christians are involved in all kinds of warfare to defeat the enemies of their destiny but only few receive total victory. The number of hours you spend in prayers does not automatically guarantee victory; the real key to total victory is identifying the specific enemy to deal with. Proper identification of the strong man through its characteristics will help us fight and defeat them once and for all. If you don't have this information, you will not only waste your resources, you will also waste your life.

Having given this background information, I want to let you know that there are four principal strong men you must conquer, for you to manifest destiny fully and in time. These four enemies are on assignment to stop you from reaching your goal in life. They come in different forms and may not bear the same names like they did in the Bible, but a little explanation on each of them will give you a better insight into their activities. These four enemies are the spirits of Goliath, Pharaoh, Herod and Jezebel.

THREE

DEMYSTIFYING THE SPIRIT OF GOLIATH

Chapter Three

"

The devil sends out the spirit of fear whenever he wants to finish off his opponent. Why? Because the devil is afraid of you.

"

Chapter Three

DEMYSTIFYING THE SPIRIT OF GOLIATH

•●⬤●•

And there went out a champion out of the camp of the Philistines, named Goliath, of Gath, whose height was six cubits and a span. And he had an helmet of brass upon his head, and he was armed with a coat of mail; and the weight of the coat was five thousand shekels of brass. And he had greaves of brass upon his legs, and a target of brass between his shoulders. And the staff of his spear was like a weaver's beam; and his spear's head weighed six hundred shekels of iron: and one bearing a shield went before him. And he stood and cried unto the armies of Israel, and said unto them, Why are ye come out to set

> *your battle in array? am not I a Philistine, and ye servants to Saul? choose you a man for you, and let him come down to me. If he be able to fight with me, and to kill me, then will we be your servants: but if I prevail against him, and kill him, then shall ye be our servants, and serve us. And the Philistine said, I defy the armies of Israel this day; give me a man, that we may fight together. 1 Samuel 17: 4-10*

Goliath is a strong man that has kept many families in bondage from generation to generation. He is the power that has hindered many generations from manifesting their God given destinies. A crucial part of his assignment is to keep everyone at the same level of achievement by ensuring that no one progresses beyond a certain height. This is the spirit that has limited the progress of sons and daughters of a particular family or village.

GOLIATH ENGAGES THE FOLLOWING SERVANT SPIRITS IN ITS OPERATIONS

FEAR AND INTIMIDATION

Goliath is that giant of an obstacle that *seems* unbeatable, or impossible to defeat. The story in 1

Samuel chapter 17 contains all the clues we need to confront and overcome Goliath.

King Saul of Israel had been fighting tooth and nail for most of his life to secure every inch of the Promised Land. Even though the land was promised, taking possession of it did not come easy. Indeed, most promised lands are like that - we have to work hard to secure them.

> *Rise ye up, take your journey, and pass over the river Arnon: behold, I HAVE GIVEN INTO THINE HAND SIHON THE AMORITE, king of Heshbon, and his land: BEGIN TO POSSESS IT, AND CONTEND WITH HIM IN BATTLE. Deut. 2:24*

Ever since the day Joshua took over the leadership baton of Israel from Moses, the fight had been on. On that first day when they crossed the Jordan River to head westward to their promised homeland, there was no welcome sign saying, "Welcome to the Promised Land!" rather they were besieged with battles upon battles!

We would have expected God to say, *I have given into thine hand Sihon, the Amorite, King of Heshbon, and his land, go and possess it*. No! You must fight for it because the devil does not give up easily even though he knows he will eventually lose the battle.

The Philistines were gaining the upper hand in this particular war and King Saul was beginning to despair. The Philistines had unveiled their "master" weapon - a terrifying nine foot nine giant named Goliath. This powerful, *fearsome* creature came out daily, taunting the Israelites, issuing a challenge that had King Saul's army cringing behind their shields.

There wasn't a soldier in the camp who wanted to take on Goliath. *Fear* and despair took hold of all the valiant soldiers in the camp and ate away at the courage of every man. Each day, Goliath looked bigger and the soldiers of Saul felt smaller.

On a particular day, Goliath began hurling insults at the soldiers of Israel as usual, as he challenged them to a fight. Little did he know that a young lad had been anointed to bring him down that same day.

> *Goliath stood and shouted to the ranks of Israel, "Why do you come out and line up for battle? Am I not a Philistine, and are you not the servants of Saul? Choose a man and have him come down to me. If he is able to fight and kill me, we will become your subjects; but if I overcome*

> *him and kill him, you will become our subjects and serve us." Then the Philistine said, "This day I defy the ranks of Israel! Give me a man and let us fight each other." On hearing the Philistine's words, Saul and all the Israelites were DISMAYED AND TERRIFIED.*

After hearing these threats, an adolescent shepherd boy named David looked around and asked "Who is this person who is insulting the armies of God?" He wasn't afraid of the Philistine giant. And that's one of the biggest secrets in defeating your Goliath.

Before you can kill Goliath, you must kill fear! The truth is that the fear of Goliath is usually more paralyzing than Goliath himself.

Satan sends out the spirit of fear whenever he wants to finish off his opponent. Why? Because the devil himself is full of fear. You can't give what you don't have hence, since the devil sends out fear, it means that he himself is full of fear - he is afraid of you!

David said to Saul, "Let no one lose heart on account of this Philistine; your servant will go and fight him." But king *Saul replied;*

> *"You are not able to go out against this Philistine and fight*

> *him; you are only a boy, and he has been a fighting man from his youth." But David said to Saul, "Your servant has been keeping his father's sheep. When a lion or a bear came and carried off a sheep from the flock, I went after it, struck it and rescued the sheep from its mouth. When it turned on me, I seized it by its hair, struck it and killed it. Your servant has killed both the lion and the bear; this uncircumcised Philistine will be like one of them, because he has defied the armies of the living God. The LORD who delivered me from the paw of the lion and the paw of the bear will deliver me from the hand of this Philistine." Saul said to David, "Go, and the LORD be with you" (1 Samuel 17:32-37).*

Goliath is that force responsible for every defeat anyone in your family or probably in your generation has suffered. This strong man called Goliath has a track record of killing anyone and everyone that has ever crossed its path, hence nobody wants to dare confront or challenge him again. In fact, other members of your family who have accepted their fate would even advise you against attempting to confront him. They will give you countless examples of people who dared confront the family deity or whatever is the force of limitation and how they were thoroughly dealt with. This information ends up creating so much fear in you and fear makes you lose heart!

But the truth is this, and you must never forget these words - *Every great thing you desire is on the other side of fear.* If you can conquer your fears, you can conquer your Goliath. Fear is the veil between the natural and the supernatural. Many times, what we fear is only a mirage; if you will dare to take steps toward it, you will discover that it does not really exist.

VOICES OF OPPOSITION

When Goliath is after your life, you will begin to hear both external and internal voices of opposition, telling you how impossible and hopeless your situation is. These voices tell you how inadequate and unprepared you are to confront your Goliath, they bombard you with terrifying stories about what happened to those who attempted to achieve what you are trying to do now. The voices magnify your weaknesses and shortcomings so you can give up on your dreams and aspirations. They show you in your mind how big your problems are and how small you are to tackle them. I am talking about voices in your mind that magnify your challenges beyond proportion so you can feel overwhelmed and helpless. But you must do what David did, you must turn away from those voices and forge ahead with your dream.

DOUBT.

Sometimes you may find yourself facing a terrible situation that can make you doubt even your salvation. This is simply because satan, through this spirit is trying hard to make you lose faith and hope in God so he can utterly finish you. The devil knows that as long as you are standing in faith, God is happy with you, but if he can get you to give up your faith in God and resort either to self-help, to a man or to a false god, then he can destroy you totally. *This was what Goliath was trying to achieve when he asked the armies of Israel to provide him a man. The daily challenge was targeted at emphasizing the disadvantage of the Israelites and making them lose confidence in their God.*

DIABOLISM

Goliath is a diabolic strong man that works with the witchcraft powers of your father's house.

In 1 Samuel chapter 17, when Goliath saw that David had crossed the threshold of fear, he became terrified and cursed David by his gods. Hallelujah!

I prophesy, by reason of the knowledge you have

gained in this book, that strongman in your father's house that might have defeated everybody else now becomes afraid of you, in the mighty name of Jesus. When Goliath saw that David advanced towards him with the kind of boldness he had not seen in any of the soldiers of Israel since the last forty days, he became so afraid that he invoked the powers of his god against David. You don't call on your god to help you fight an easy opponent. You invoke the help of your god when the battle has turned against you and defeat stares you in the face, and that is exactly what Goliath did.

> *And the Philistine said unto David, Am I a dog, that thou comest to me with staves? And the Philistine cursed David by his gods. 1Sam 17:43*

By his choice of weapon, David communicated to Goliath how inconsequential an opponent he was. And that's how you must also deal with your Goliath.

So David, instead of putting on an armor and a sword, chose to dress simply, carrying only a sling in his hand and (with five smooth stones that he collected from the stream) he was ready for war!

He brought out only one stone, slung it and it struck Goliath on the forehead and killed him. The inexperienced young man had just won a major victory in his first human combat and with no less an opponent!

David's confidence in this fight was not in the standard resources. It was neither in the armor of Saul nor the support of the Israelite army, but in God. If he had subjected himself to the average thinking pattern, he would have died in that battle field but because he was able to think outside the box, the Lord his God gave him strength to defeat an obviously stronger enemy.

Goliath is that enemy you must conquer before you rise to limelight. He is the major barrier to your next level of settlement. He is that giant that some other persons in your family who though know the truth, are nonetheless afraid to confront.

In times of confrontation with Goliath, our first line of defense is our relationship with God. God has all power and He can deliver us, therefore we must trust in His strength, no matter what others may consider the best way out of our difficulties.

Listen to what David said when he confronted Goliath: *"You come against me with sword and spear and javelin, but I come against you in the name of the LORD Almighty, the God of the armies of Israel, whom you have defied. This day the LORD will hand you over to me, and I'll strike you down and cut off your head. Today I will give the carcasses of the Philistine army to the birds of the air and the beasts of the earth, and the whole world will know that there is a God in Israel. All those gathered here will know that it is not by sword or spear that the LORD saves; for the battle is the LORD's, and he will give all of you into our hands*" (vs. 45-47).

When you compare yourself to your Goliath, it is easy to become fearful. But when you compare your Goliath to your God, then you realize that you have nothing, absolutely nothing to fear.

MANIPULATIONS

Goliath is that giant that wants everybody else to remain ants so he can successfully manipulate their destinies. Great men and women have been stranded on the highway of success due to insurmountable struggles and battles of life. Goliath magnifies himself in your mind, tells you how huge and difficult your challenges are and how small and incompetent you are to handle them. In order for Goliath to achieve his sinister agenda against you, he employs the manipulation of witchcraft spirits.

NONSTOP BATTLES

This spirit keeps you on your toes with every manner of battles just to distract you from paying attention to your destiny. In 1 Kings 5:1-5, David could not achieve his dreams of building a house for his God because of the ceaseless battles he was engaged in all through his life. He had a great vision but could not achieve it because this spirit engaged him in battles on every side. He had battles with different nations, battles with morality, battles in his family even battles with close associates, (his son and his prophet, Ahitophel)

When the spirit of Goliath occupies you with such myriad of battles, it becomes easy for you to lose focus and direction.

> *And Hiram king of Tyre sent his servants unto Solomon; for he had heard that they had anointed him king in the room of his father: for Hiram was ever a lover of David. And Solomon sent to Hiram, saying, Thou knowest how that David my father could not build an house unto the name of the LORD his God for the wars which were about him on every side, until the LORD put them under the soles of his feet. But now the LORD my God hath given me rest on every side, so that there is neither adversary nor evil occurrent. And, behold, I purpose to build an house unto the name of the LORD my God, as the LORD spake unto David my father,*

> *saying, Thy son, whom I will set upon thy throne in thy room, he shall build an house unto my name. 1 Kings 5:1-5*

This is the picture of many people today who are burdened with divers challenges. As they are getting out of one problem, another one shows up, then another and another.

You need to aggressively confront this spirit. Until David showed up and killed him, Saul and his army remained in the battle field for forty days without making any progress. Can I shock you? The forty days the armies of Israel wasted in the battle field could be forty years or even a life time for some people, unless they rise up in warfare.

YOU CAN BE FREE

Child of God, it took a man with the oil of victory to change the narrative for Israel. You are that man or woman God is waiting for to use to destroy this strong man in your family.

You are the David of your family who God will use to kill that Goliath that has hindered everyone in your family until now. God has anointed your head with oil and this Goliath will die in your hand!

The account recorded in the book of Judges chapter

14, indicates that the ferocious lion at Timnath had always denied Samson's generation access beyond the vineyards. Indeed, Samson was all alone on this fateful journey when the lion launched an attack against him, thus suggesting that his parents who had set off on the journey with him, did (could) not get to the vineyards of Timnath with him. But in verses 5-9 Samson, by the Spirit of God, put up a valiant fight, defeated this lion and secured a generational victory.

> *Then went Samson down, and his father and his mother, to Timnath, and came to the vineyards of Timnath: and, behold, a young lion roared against him. And the Spirit of the LORD came mightily upon him, and he rent him as he would have rent a kid, and he had nothing in his hand: but he told not his father or his mother what he had done. And he went down, and talked with the woman; and she pleased Samson well. And after a time he returned to take her, and he turned aside to see the carcass of the lion: and, behold, there was a swarm of bees and honey in the carcass of the lion. And he took thereof in his hands, and went on eating, and came to*

his father and mother, and he gave them, and they did eat: but he told not them that he had taken the honey out of the carcass of the lion. Judges 14:5-9

The lion had always stopped Samson's generation at the border of Timnath and hindered them access to whatever treasures lay at the other side, but when anointed Samson appeared and killed the lion, he broke that barrier and his family was at liberty to access their blessings. Shortly after this great victory, Samson was able to eat honey from the carcass of the same lion and he gave some to his parents to eat also. Victory is sweet! His parents tasted sweetness for the first time because their son took responsibility for the deliverance of his family.

This book in your hands is a testimony that you are the one chosen by God to restore the glory which Goliath has stolen and restore sweetness to your family.

Let me quickly tell you this, if you fight for your deliverance alone without fighting for that of your siblings and your entire family, you will surely be delivered but by the time the whole family depends on you for virtually all their needs, your situation will be worse than when you too, were in bondage with them.

The same authority you will use to break yourself free can be wielded to set your entire family free. When David asked Saul's men concerning the reward for killing Goliath, he was told that the family of whoever kills Goliath will be tax free in Israel and that became an additional motivation for the young man. You too, ought to include your family in your quest for complete deliverance because **every great man thinks not only about himself but also about the emancipation of his family and generation.**

Make up your mind to conquer Goliath because until he dies, you will have no rest.

FOUR

DEMYSTIFYING THE SPIRIT OF PHARAOH

Chapter Four

"

Pharaoh is the spirit that prolongs your suffering beyond the limit you can bear in order to frustrate you and make you to question the authenticity of the Word of God.

"

Chapter Four

DEMYSTIFYING THE SPIRIT OF PHARAOH

•●●●•

And Pharaoh called unto Moses, and said, Go ye, serve the LORD; only let your flocks and your herds be stayed: let your little ones also go with you. And Moses said, Thou must give us also sacrifices and burnt offerings, that we may sacrifice unto the LORD our God. Our cattle also shall go with us; there shall not an hoof be left behind; for thereof must we take to serve the LORD our God; and we know not with what we must serve the LORD, until we come thither. But the LORD hardened Pharaoh's heart, and he would not let them go. And Pharaoh said unto him, Get thee from me, take heed to thyself, see my face no more; for in that day thou seest my face thou shalt die. And Moses said, Thou hast spoken well, I will see thy face again no more. Exodus 10:24-29

HOW TO IDENTIFY THE SPIRIT OF PHARAOH

A correct identification of the strong man responsible for an affliction is the first step to guaranteed and complete freedom from its clutches. Ascribing the operations of one evil spirit to another is like a patient wrongly diagnosed in a medical facility; such a patient will spend precious time and resources treating the wrong ailment and they may develop complications or even lose their life.

Below are signs and symptoms you will observe when the spirit of Pharaoh is in operation:

PROLONGED BONDAGE AND DELAY

Pharaoh is the principality in charge of prolonged bondage. He is the power behind the mystery of delay. In the scriptures above, Pharaoh prolonged the servitude of the Hebrews in Egypt for thirty more years beyond God's agreement of four hundred years with Abraham.

And he said unto Abram, Know of a surety that thy seed shall be a stranger in a land that is not theirs, and shall serve them; and they shall afflict them four hundred years; And also that nation, whom they shall serve, will I judge: and afterward shall they come out with great substance. Gen. 15:13-14.

There are multitudes of people whose cycle of challenges and trials should have long ended but the spirit of Pharaoh has prolonged their pains and tears. Some have died in the process, while some have sought for help from strange places in order to end their travails.

This spirit takes advantage of people's ignorance of the source of their problems to prolong their sufferings and in the process, create doubt and discourage them from trusting God. Why? **The *ignorance* of the oppressed is the strength of the oppressor.**

Moses and the Hebrews did not understand that the journey into Egypt began with the blood on the altar of covenant between God and Abraham in Gen. 15: 2-14: 17 & 18.

In his quest to deliver the children of Israel, Moses

came against Pharaoh and all the gods of Egypt with various signs and wonders but Pharaoh would not let them go. Nine notable devastating wonders took place in Egypt, yet Pharaoh did not succumb until God revealed to Moses that it would take the power of sacrifice and blood to obtain freedom for the Hebrews (Exodus 12:1-13). The reason was because the covenant that led to their four hundred years of bondage was made by blood. When the people sacrificed their lambs and applied the blood on their lintel and door posts, God sped up action that same night and ended their slavery of four hundred and thirty years by a mighty hand.

My point is that the persistent miseries in many lives are products of mysteries from past generations that they are ignorant of. It will take the power of the Holy Spirit to unveil the mysteries before total freedom can be obtained.

Pharaoh is the spirit that prolongs your suffering beyond the limit you can bear in order to frustrate you and make you question the authenticity of the Word of God.

This spirit specializes in making sure you don't get hundred percent of your freedom. When subjected to intense prayers, he bows and grants you partial and/or temporary relief only to return with fresh complications. He fights to ensure you get only limited deliverance.

> *And when the LORD saw that they humbled themselves, the ord of the LORD came to Shemaiah, saying, They have humbled themselves; therefore I will not destroy them, but I will grant them SOME DELIVERANCE; and my wrath shall not be poured out upon Jerusalem by the hand of Shishak. 2Chron. 12:7*

But when you conquer this spirit, you experience GREAT DELIVERANCE.

> *And they set themselves in the midst of that parcel, and delivered it, and slew the Philistines; and the LORD saved them by a GREAT DELIVERANCE. 1 Chron. 11:14*

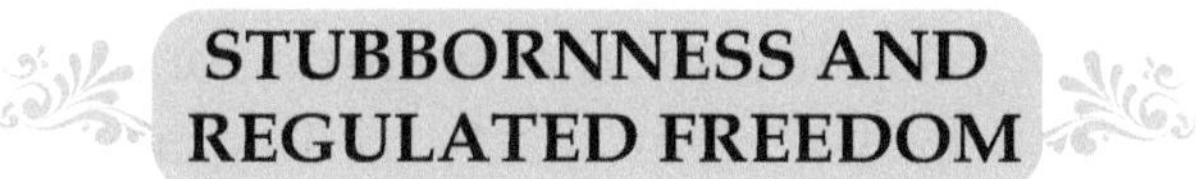

STUBBORNNESS AND REGULATED FREEDOM

Pharaoh is that spirit that ensures that you don't go far in life. He is the spirit of limitation and regulated freedom. As soon as you are about to celebrate, something tragic happens to take away your joy.

And Pharaoh called unto Moses, and said, Go ye, serve the LORD; only let your flocks and your herds be stayed: let your little ones also go with you. Exodus 10:24

Pharaoh is a representation of the spirit of bondage, slavery, oppression, stubbornness, denial, recurring affliction, and hard-heartedness. He refused to let the Israelites go even after mighty miraculous demonstrations. And when he finally succumbed to a Superior Power and let them go, he soon changed his mind and pursued after them.

If you're confronted with situations and problems that refuse to go even after intense prayers, fasting, prophetic declarations, and several godly people praying for you, then you may be facing a situation orchestrated by the spirit of Pharaoh.

The spirit of Pharaoh is a very stubborn spirit that you must confront if you are serious about moving to the next level of your life. God is waiting for you to cry out to Him because He is ready to disgrace and bury that Pharaoh on your behalf.

Son of man, set your face against Pharaoh king of Egypt, and prophesy against him, and against all Egypt. Speak, and say, 'Thus says the Lord God: "Behold, I am against you, O Pharaoh king of Egypt, O great monster who lies in the midst of his rivers, Who has said, 'My river is my own; I have made it for myself.' But I will put hooks in your jaws, and cause the fish of your rivers to stick to your scales; I will bring you up out of the midst of your rivers, and all the fish in your rivers will stick to your scales. I will leave you in the wilderness, you and all the fish of your rivers; you shall fall on the open field; You shall not be picked up or gathered. I have given you as food to the beasts of the field and the birds of the heavens. Ezekiel 29:2-5

AFFLICTION FROM CHILDHOOD

Afflictions, pains and specific sufferings that start in childhood and continue into one's adulthood are orchestrated by the spirit of Pharaoh. Such afflictions are intended to thwart a person's destiny, to prevent the person from amounting to anything in life. These afflictions usually defy prayers and efforts at a solution, until God's revelation, power, and judgments are invoked.

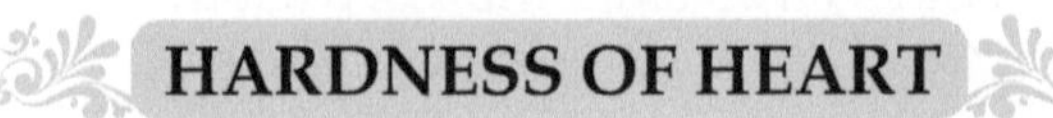

HARDNESS OF HEART

If you're dealing with someone who displays unusual hardness of heart, that person may be under the influence of the spirit of Pharaoh. Many hardened criminals are under the control of this spirit. Pharaoh's heart was so hardened that the Lord had to bombard him with ten dangerous plagues, and even after the ten plagues, he remained hardened until he was buried alive in the Red Sea.

Some problems and situations in your life need to be buried in the Red Sea!

RECURRENT AFFLICTION

Another thing that the spirit of Pharaoh causes is recurrent affliction. This type of affliction gets resolved but then it keeps coming back again and again. To compound matters, the problem usually gets worse each time it returns, each episode proving more difficult to resolve than the previous one. That is a sign of the spirit of Pharaoh at work.

INCREASE IN SUFFERING AT THE THRESHOLD OF DELIVERANCE

The spirit of Pharaoh increases the level of sufferings when they sense that their captives are about to gain their freedom. This may be hard to believe, but there are some people who pray for deliverance from a particular problem only for their situation to go from bad to worse mysteriously.

It is however encouraging to know that it's not God who increases their suffering. These demons know when a person is tired of their situation and wants to be free. They then go all out to make you feel that the prayers you are making are the reason the problems are increasing. They are the spirits of Pharaoh.

MOCKERY AND ARROGANCE

The spirit of Pharaoh is also the spirit of mockery. This spirit represents enemies who believe they can do anything to you and nothing will happen to them. When presented with the Word or the name of God, they would mock and make jests about it. He makes you a ridicule before others because the more you pray and fast, the more he intensifies your suffering. He only bows and gives up when you make painful sacrifices which we shall be looking at in subsequent chapters.

When Moses went to Pharaoh in Exodus 5:2 and pleaded for him to let the Israelites go, he responded,

> *"Who is the Lord that I should obey His voice to let Israel go? I do not know the Lord, nor will I let Israel go."*

That's another way of saying, *"I have no regard for your God; I don't believe He can do anything to me. I'll not stop oppressing you."* It was only in the midst of the Red Sea that Pharaoh finally let the Israelites go and that was at a point where there was absolutely nothing he could do anymore to stop them, since he was gasping for his own life.

I pray for you, dear reader, **every stubborn enemy of your life shall be buried in the Red Sea today, in the mighty name of Jesus!** Please understand that the enemy won't let you go because you pray, *"Lord, I'm suffering so much. Why will You let my enemies laugh at me? I need help."* No! You have to demand justice and begin to release fire from heaven to swallow every projection of the spirit of Pharaoh against your life and family!

God has sent us Christ, and in His death and resurrection lies all the help we'll ever need.

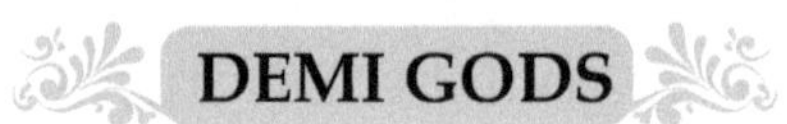

DEMI GODS

In ancient Egypt, Pharaohs were perceived to be gods so they were worshipped. They operated a dictatorial, not a democratic system of government.

It is the spirit of Pharaoh that possesses all modern day dictators. If you're in a relationship where your partner displays dictatorial tendencies, you need to take authority against the spirit of Pharaoh. If you work with a boss who is a dictator, take authority against the spirit of Pharaoh in that company.

The goal of every Pharaoh is to be worshipped and served without question. Don't go fighting the person physically, begin to take authority against the demons.

PURSUERS UNTO DEATH

A lady once told me about a strange bird that followed her wherever she went. No one else but her sees this strange bird and it followed her stubbornly from one city to another until she had to park out of her husband's house.

A lot of people are being pursued by what they don't know, and as a result, many things happen in their lives that they can't explain. Their spiritual lives never catch fire because their pursuers create all manner of distractions, sometimes even in the form of pleasures and false hopes that keep their victims perpetually in their grip. Their marriages are always having a crisis; their health is always suffering; their finances are always in disarray.

The spirit of Pharaoh is a stubborn pursuer whose goal is to punish you with hard labour until you die.

I pray for you reading this book, that God will arise and swallow all stubborn pursuers of your life and

destiny, in Jesus' name.

INCREASED BURDEN

It is this spirit that multiplies your burden and increases your pains as soon as you begin to seek for your freedom. This is the reason why some people's cases become complicated after deliverance ministrations because they did not deal with the root of their problems.

Pharaoh increases your responsibility and denies you the means of meeting them. He increases your expenditure and diminishes your income.

> *And Pharaoh said, Behold, the people of the land now are many, and ye make them rest from their burdens. And Pharaoh commanded the same day the taskmasters of the people, and their officers, saying, Ye shall no more give the people straw to make brick, as heretofore: let them go and gather straw for themselves. And the tale of the bricks, which they did make heretofore, ye shall lay upon them; ye shall not diminish ought thereof: for they be idle; therefore they cry, saying, Let us go and*

sacrifice to our God. Let there more work be laid upon the men, that they may labour therein; and let them not regard vain words. And the taskmasters of the people went out, and their officers, and they spake to the people, saying, Thus saith Pharaoh, I will not give you straw. Go ye, get you straw where ye can find it: yet not ought of your work shall be diminished. So the people were scattered abroad throughout all the land of Egypt to gather stubble instead of straw. And the taskmasters hasted them, saying, Fulfil your works, your daily tasks, as when there was straw. Exodus 5:5-13

EXPLOITATION

This spirit uses your talent, skills, energy and potentials for his benefit. You know this is what you are going through when your labour yields benefits to others who end up using you. Your ideas improve other people's lives but not yours, you show others how to succeed but you have nothing to show for all your wealth of knowledge. People take your ideas, make much from them and in return, give you peanuts.

FIVE

DEMYSTIFYING THE SPIRIT OF HEROD

Chapter Five

"

Herod is the spirit that
Attacks anything that
Will benefit your future

"

Chapter Five

DEMYSTIFYING THE SPIRIT OF HEROD

•●⬤●•

Now about that time Herod the king stretched forth his hands to vex certain of the church. And he killed James the brother of John with the sword. And because he saw it pleased the Jews, he proceeded further to take Peter also. (Then were the days of unleavened bread.) And when he had apprehended him, he put him in prison, and delivered him to four quaternions of soldiers to keep him; intending after Easter to bring him forth to the people. Peter therefore was kept in prison: but prayer was made without ceasing of the church unto God for him. Hebrews 12:1-5

The name Herod means "son of the hero" or "descendant of the hero"; laying claims to a significant beginning. You also have a significant beginning because God made you, and He has kept you alive in this season for a purpose. Even if your earlier years in life were not favourable and your present condition is unpleasant, there is still hope that you can finish well.

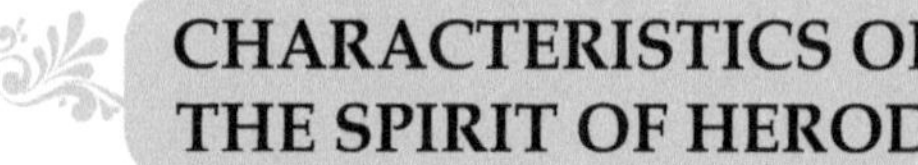

CHARACTERISTICS OF THE SPIRIT OF HEROD

DESTROYER OF GREAT POTENTIALS
(Matthew 2:1-19)

Herod works to further weaken the weak and destroy the helpless.

The spirit that worked in Athaliah and Herod are similar. Both represent oppression, rejection, stagnation and attempts to stifle your greatness in life, career, family and destiny.

In 2 Kings chapter 11, after her son died, Athaliah, moved by this wicked spirit, went on to destroy her own grandchildren, in order that she might realize her evil way. One of her grandchildren, Joash, was miraculously delivered from her scheme of death as he was snatched from among those to be slain. Thereafter, he was hidden for six years while the crown which was meant for him was withheld and Athaliah, his grandmother reigned in his stead. Even Jesus, though the Son of God, had to be hidden for some years until God by His mighty hand destroyed

Herod. Until Athaliah and Herod were destroyed, neither Joash nor Jesus in their time, could fulfill their destiny.

REPRESSIVE

> *The same day there came certain of the Pharisees, saying unto him, Get thee out, and depart hence: for Herod will kill thee. Luke 13:31*

In Mark 6:14-32, Herod had taken his brother, Phillip's wife. They probably lived close to each other; but even with his brother close by, he still went ahead and took his wife and daughter and started living with them. The emotional and psychological trauma of this experience probably killed the man in Phillip. Therein lies the goal of Herod - to silence and to kill.

In Acts 12:1-19, Herod killed Apostle James, the head of the church, and went further to arrest Apostle Peter, being the next in command. He had him kept in the inner prison with sixteen soldiers guarding him until the end of the feast when he would be executed.

ENEMY OF HEADS OF FAMILIES

His target is to destroy the bread winner of the family so that his children would miss their destiny. There are a good number of people roaming the streets today who were born in affluence but one tragedy or another took out the bread winner and that was how their destiny went into the grave! Some who were in tertiary institutions could not complete their study as a result of the death of their parents or bread winner. It is the spirit of Herod at work. He locates leaders of the family and afflicts them with deadly disease that incapacitates them from achieving their dreams for their family. He arrests potential leaders and puts them in the prison of drug addiction, prostitution, pornography, adultery, masturbation, alcoholism, polygamy, idolatry, cultism and similar vices so they won't be able to fulfill destiny.

SNUFFS OUT BRIGHT PROSPECTS

King Herod in the Bible was known for his wicked activities against humanity. In his attempt to eliminate baby Jesus, he killed thousands of innocent children from ages zero to two years.

His target was to kill and destroy the future. He kills anything that will project you in future. He kills businesses in their prime through mismanagements, wrong partnerships and investments. He kills marriages and relationships that have a bright future through *avoidable* misunderstandings and constant conflicts.

He kills great ministries at their early stage by

attacking the moral life, finances and marriage of the sent man. He is the spirit that aborts dreams, visions and goals in life. He targets and kills anybody who has a bright future in the family so that the family will remain in poverty.

Your greatness is a threat to Herod and he fights with the weapon of death. You must destroy this enemy if you desire a colourful future.

WEAKENS POSITIVE RESOLVE

A careful observation in your life may reveal to you, certain people who habitually attempt to weaken you just when you have resolved to do something good or take a big step. These people may even be "friends" or family members who may claim to be looking out for your good but all they do is show you all the negative aspects of the good you want to achieve. In the case of Jesus, Herod sent the familiar enemies, the Pharisees to threaten Him, but Jesus kept the faith - He did not waver in His stance, preaching the good news healing and loosing the bound. He remained focused on His ministry. As you seek to fulfill your glorious destiny, never allow any negative thing you hear or see to discourage or distract you, rather, strengthen your feeble knees and hands. Our God is a Tower of strength and He will strengthen you.

HEROD IS A FOX

*And he said to them, **GO YE,***

AND TELL THAT FOX,
Behold, I cast out devils, and I do cures today and tomorrow, and the third day I shall be perfected.
Luke 13:32

Why did Jesus call Herod a fox? Foxes are cunning, deceitful cheats, who prey on the good. I believe that Herod's brother, Phillip, did not know in time that he was scheming for his wife, otherwise he would have taken steps to secure his family rather than allow a fox disintegrate his family and reduce him to nothing.

I pray for you child of God, that God will expose any foxes around your life and shield you from their deceitfulness, in Jesus' name.

A fox is a wild animal of the dog family with reddish brown or grey fur and bushy tail. He is carnivorous, has a pointed muzzle and large ears. Foxes are found throughout most of the world. They hunt alone, mainly at night, relying on their cunningness and an acute sense of hearing and smell. To call someone a fox is a metaphor that describes someone who is sly, and a trickster who easily outwits others through deception.

It is my sincere prayer for you that God will disgrace every Herod around your life, family and ministry, in Jesus' mighty name.

SIX

DEMYSTIFYING THE SPIRIT OF JEZEBEL

Chapter Six

"

The spirit of Jezebel works against legitimate authority as she manipulates those in authority with gifts, seductions and enticing words.

"

Chapter Six

DEMYSTIFYING THE SPIRIT OF JEZEBEL

•●⬤●•

And Ahab told Jezebel all that Elijah had done, and withal how he had slain all the prophets with the sword. Then Jezebel sent a messenger unto Elijah, saying, So let the gods do to me, and more also, if I make not thy life as the life of one of them by tomorrow about this time. And when he saw that, he arose, and went for his life, and came to Beersheba, which belongeth to Judah, and left his servant there. But he himself went a day's journey into the wilderness, and came and sat down under a juniper tree: and he requested for himself that he might die; and said, It is enough;

now, O LORD, take away my life; for I am not better than my fathers. 1Kings 19:1-4

Without question, the spirit of Jezebel is the vilest, most cunning, and seductive evil spirit in satan's hierarchy. This is because of its seemingly harmless appearance and the "slimy" style it employs to fraternize with its targeted victim. Though named after a female, this spirit can possess either males or females.

JEZEBEL ALERTS

DESTROYER OF THE GOOD

This evil spirit has been responsible, not only for tearing down glorious destinies, Christian ministers and ministries, but it is also responsible for breaking up many marriages, friendships and businesses. She is involved in anything that brings tears, sorrow, agony and bloodshed, along with getting people to commit cold-blooded murders and suicides.

CONTROL FREAK

The name "Jezebel" was made popular by an infamous queen in the Old Testament. While Ahab her husband was the king, Jezebel was the one calling the shots! Ahab was simply a figure head king whereas Jezebel was the real ruler. Many times, in some organizations, the real leader who influences major decisions acts from behind the scene and it is an undisputable fact that anyone who has the ears of the leader is a very strong force to reckon with - that is Jezebel!

Jezebel is a very strong spirit that works behind the scene to control the affairs of families, villages, individuals etc. The spirit of Jezebel offers immediate gratification with future complications. It is a witchcraft spirit that controls, dominates and manipulates people to go against God.

STRIPS MEN OF THEIR MANLINESS

This spirit attacks the finances of men and makes them utterly dependent on women for economic sustenance. Interestingly, no woman can offer total financial support to her husband for any reasonable period of time without showing some attitudinal traits of insubordination whether consciously or unconsciously. If you study some African and even American cities, you will discover that it is the women that do legitimate work there while the men loiter about preoccupied with diverse vices, consuming drugs and illicit substances.

It is the spirit of Jezebel that makes a man financially useless so that his authority in the home will be undermined. When this spirit is set to destroy a home, it cripples the authority of the man, and when it wants to besiege a nation, it attacks the economic power of the men in that nation. Jezebel's main grouse is this - *she doesn't want men to be men indeed*!

In fact, some governments have been bewitched to legally favour the feminine cause against men. For instance, whenever there is a squabble in the home, it is the man that the government throws out of the home, thereby rendering him homeless. Jezebel takes what is rightfully yours and gives it to another person.

USURPS AUTHORITY

The spirit of Jezebel empowers the woman to usurp the authority which God ordained for the man. This is the spirit behind all the gender equality campaigns you see and hear about everywhere. In a marriage, if the woman is the one with this spirit, she will deliberately try and usurp her husband's authority as the head of the household. She will also attempt to totally take over from him as the spiritual head of the house, whereas, the immortal and all-knowing God in His infinite wisdom, has made the man the head and a*nything that has more than one head is a beast*!

If you look critically at some families, you will notice that the men are economically unproductive while the women are the ones catering for them even up to the clothes on their backs; and this is irrespective of the position of the men in the family. When there is any major project to be embarked upon in the family, until the women rise up, nothing substantial will be achieved beyond empty boastings and useless talks from the men folk. If the women don't move, nothing moves.

If you are not careful, no matter how financially stable you are before marrying from such a family, sooner or later after the marriage, you will join the queue of economically useless men.

The spirit of Jezebel works against legitimate authority as she manipulates those in authority with gifts, seductions and enticing words.

ATTACKS SOURCES OF INCOME.

This spirit will try to seize your source of income just like it did to Naboth and if you ignorantly attempt to resist through physical means by resorting to your fists or logic without engaging in spiritual warfare, the punishment is death. This wicked spirit knows that when a man is crippled financially, very little or nothing can be done to salvage him.

PROPAGATES *FALSEHOOD AND LIES*

If need be, the spirit of Jezebel employs lies, false accusation and manipulation to eliminate its target. It will interest you to know that the people who lied against Naboth to set him up were men from his city who probably had long standing and cordial relationships with him, until they encountered Jezebel. Naboth was doing fine in every way until Jezebel showed up. He was man enough to resist even the king from illegal possession of his means of income and he actually succeeded in his noble fight - until Jezebel showed up! In line with her propagation of falsehood, this is the spirit behind false prophets and prophecies. It is the spirit that sponsors false teachings and doctrines. You really need to kill Jezebel now!

FIGHTS THE ANOINTING AND THE ANOINTED

This spirit has been successful over the years in bringing down many anointed children of God because it has the ability to draw people into its well spun webs, and before the victim realizes what they have been caught up in, it moves in to either kill the person, or try and completely take the person out of whatever their calling might be in the Lord. This is the spirit at work when you hear that a certain man of God has abandoned their ministry and gone after a strange woman. Some remain in ministry but they are plagued by scandal after scandal, usually bordering on one act/form of immorality or another. The human embodiment of this spirit was a ruling queen who during her reign, massacred many of God's prophets in cold blood.

SELF-SEEKING

As a result of having a rather high energy level and being seductive in nature, the Jezebel spirit will usually possess a smart, intelligent and attractive physical representative to carry out its selfish agenda. Not that it won't attempt to possess a less attractive person, but the physically attractive ones are its chief target.

I believe the reason this spirit likes to target these kind of people is because of its love for attention and prominence. As a result, wherever this spirit is found, she looks for personalities that she can manipulate to climb to a place of prominence where she can be easily noticed.

The spirit of Jezebel does not marry a man and then seek to grow with him, on the contrary, she would rather marry an already made man who can facilitate her self-centered ambitions.

If this spirit is working amidst a prayer group, it will try and work its way to the top so it can become the leader of the group. If it is working within a church, it will try and work its way to the top to become the right hand man of the senior pastor, and from there, start to directly attack him so it can completely knock him out of God's call on his life.

SEDUCTIONS

Remember what Delilah did with Samson? Her mission and manner of operation points to the possibility that Delilah may have had this spirit operating in her. Through her very seductive charms and allure, she completely brought down the man with probably the greatest physical strength by reason of God's anointing. She bombarded him though seductively, with incessant pressure to reveal the secret of his life to her, until there was no more strength left in him to resist her!

This is why this kind of spirit is deadly, because it employs sexual seduction, to gets its way and eventually bring down the person or ministry targeted.

As we all know, many men are easily lured into illicit affairs by pretty women. Some men even confess that women know how to get a man "wrapped around their little fingers". Again and again, we have heard and seen great men helplessly fall victim to this spirit. Sex is a very powerful weapon, and this demon employs it whenever it can with its male or female agents to destroy its victim.

EXPLOITS PEOPLE'S WEAK POINTS

One of the things I have noticed about this spirit is that it is very good at playing mind games with people. It targets the weak spots and jugular veins of its victim so it can demoralize and bring them down.

It will attack your self-confidence, self-esteem and even your spiritual calling. The spirit of Jezebel will attack your personality traits, both good and bad, in an attempt to convince you that you are nobody and that you will never amount to anything worthwhile in this life. The aim of this mind game is to make you feel worthless and if it succeeds, it won't be long and you will actually become worthless because *as a man thinketh in his heart, so is he.*

This (feeling of) worthlessness graduates into depression with its accompanying signs of confusion, indecisiveness and disorientation.

In other words, this evil spirit will try to suck the life out of you and tear you down every way it can so you can no longer function in your calling for the Lord.

One of her earliest victims, Prophet Elijah himself, was so distraught and depressed after coming into contact with Queen Jezebel, that he wanted to throw in the towel. It took only one sinister message from Jezebel and the fiery prophet actually prayed God to take his life, but God intervened in the matter by strengthening him through an angel and then gave him a clear word of direction for the next course of action.

CRITICAL AND JUDGMENTAL

This spirit is very good at being very critical and judgmental. It will have you believing all of the lies it keeps throwing at you. She doesn't see anything good in what you do or are trying to achieve but delights in magnifying your weaknesses to undermine your strength.

This is why it is of utmost importance that you keep studying the Word of God to gain better understanding of who you are in Christ, and so that you never allow a person with this spirit to be able to bring you down like they almost did with Elijah.

Learn to speak the right words to yourself and guard your mind against "*jezebelic*" thoughts and words.

Let this part of Elijah's story be a major lesson to all of us on how far this spirit will go to literally try and get you to quit and walk out on your divine assignment. I believe a lot of the suicides we see are as a result of this spirit's evil influence over a person.

If they can attempt this with a great man of God like Elijah, then they will attempt same with anyone of us if we do not take necessary precautions.

NAGS

This is the spirit responsible for confusion and

persistent quarrels in families and wherever it is found. Over the years, I have personally witnessed several men reduced to a mere shadow of what they were destined to be by women who were operating under the influence of this spirit. These agents just kept beating the men down with verbal assaults, tearing at their self-confidence, their self-worth in God, and what they were doing in their calling.

By the time they were done with the men, many of them had lost their marriages, homes, their calling in the Lord or even their lives. **You must identify and kill the spirit of Jezebel now before it's too late.**

THE ANOINTING OF JEHU

The anointing of Jehu is the anointing that can dislodge, defeat and destroy Jezebel and her witchcraft. Even though Jezebel is the mother of witchcraft, this anointing is immune to her witchcraft seductions and mental manipulation.

> *And it came to pass, when Joram saw Jehu, that he said, Is it peace, Jehu? And he answered, What peace, so long as the whoredoms of thy mother Jezebel and her witchcrafts are so many? 2Kings 9:22*

When she heard that Jehu was coming, she quickly

ran to paint her face, showing the high level of confidence which she had in the occultic painting that she had used to manipulate others. However, upon Jehu, her witchcraft had no effect.

> *And when Jehu was come to Jezreel,* ***Jezebel heard of it; and she painted her face, and tied her head,*** *and looked out at a window. And as Jehu entered in at the gate, she said, Had Zimri peace, who slew his master? And he lifted up his face to the window, and said, Who is on my side? Who? And there looked out to him two or three eunuchs. And he said, Throw her down. So they threw her down: and some of her blood was sprinkled on the wall, and on the horses: and he trode her under foot. 2Kings 9:30-33*

When Jehu showed up, the formerly cowardly palace eunuchs were imparted by the anointing upon his life and they received courage to respond to his command to throw her down.

I release this Jehu anointing upon your life, to destroy every spirit of Jezebel at work against your life, in the name of Jesus.

SEVEN

WHO MADE THIS EVIL LAW?

Chapter Seven

"

...from the beginning
it was not so

"

Matthew 19:8

Chapter Seven

WHO MADE THIS EVIL LAW?

And Joshua called for them, and he spake unto them, saying, Wherefore have ye beguiled us, saying, We are very far from you; when ye dwell among us? Now therefore ye are cursed, and there shall none of you be freed from being bondmen, and hewers of wood and drawers of water for the house of my God. And they answered Joshua, and said, Because it was certainly told thy servants, how that the LORD thy God commanded his servant Moses to give you all the land, and to destroy all the inhabitants of the land from before you, therefore we were sore afraid of our lives because of you, and have done this thing. And now, behold, we are in thine hand: as it seemeth good and right unto thee to do unto us, do. And so did he unto them, and delivered them out of the hand of the children of Israel, that they slew them not. And Joshua made them that day hewers of wood and drawers of water for the congregation, and for the altar of the LORD, even unto this day, in the place which he should choose. Joshua 9:22-27

Life is governed by laws which are put in place to control, regulate and limit you. Some are written, while others are spoken. God's laws will not put you in bondage; only man-made laws do that.

For a divine shift to take place in your life, certain laws that have limited you must be broken. ***For any notable miracle to take place, you need to break a major law that is contrary to you.***

Mary's conception without sleeping with a man broke the law of gynecology. When an axe head floated on water, it broke the law of gravity. Lazarus' resurrection broke the law of anatomy.

The secret of victorious life therefore is identifying which and who made the law keeping you where you don't want to be. Is it God, satan or man?

Who made the laws of poverty frustrating people's efforts?

Who made the laws of barrenness?
Who made the laws of misfortune?
Who made the laws of untimely death and all other contrary laws?

We know that God is almighty and He does only good. Therefore, since it's not Him who made the evil laws, it means that whoever else made them, as God's children, we have the power to break or change them.

Every law that keeps God's children in captivity is illegal and lacks authority to function in their life except they permit it.

In Numbers 27:1-7, the daughters of Zelophehad rose up and challenged the law of inheritance in Israel. They queried the laws that excluded daughters from their father's inheritance. They were tired of the laws which denied them their portion in life and made them live like slaves in their own fatherland. They desired a change of the status-quo.

They knew their root was from Joseph the son of Jacob, the son of Isaac, the son of Abraham, and in spite of the fact that this law was accepted by the whole nation of Israel, they damned whatever the consequences might be. These five women confronted Prophet Moses, the priests, the princes, the elders and the entire congregation of Israel and demanded a change of the law.

"Why should the name of our father be done away with from among his family because he had no sons? Give unto us therefore a possession among the brethren of our father" Their question addressed their need. Perhaps your own relevant question would be: "Why should I be denied success because of my background? Why should the altars of my father's house deny me my portion in life? Why should I suffer because of what my (fore) fathers did?" **I demand a change right now!**

I decree over your life, let the wicked ancient laws of your father's house break by fire, in the name of Jesus. Amen.

Child of God, you can demand your freedom no matter who made the law working against you. When Moses heard their demand, he went to God to seek for solution and the Lord told him that He wasn't the One who made that law. He therefore commanded that their demand be met. Can you imagine that? As popularly accepted as that law was amongst the leaders and people of Israel, God wasn't the One who made it!

Are you aware that there were many like the daughters of Zelophehad who lived and died without enjoying their portions because they did not take the risk to place a demand? Until you rebel against the law that has held you captive, you may not access your freedom. You can become that agent of change in your family and generation, if only you will take the necessary risk.

Divine shifts belongs only to risk takers. If you don't sacrifice the present pleasure for your future treasure, your future will be filled with undue pressure.

God is our Maker. He made us perfect in His image and likeness; indeed everything He made is good.

> *And God saw everything that he had made, and, behold, it was very good. And the evening and the morning were the sixth day. Gen. 1:31*

Jesus said to Peter, "follow me and I will make you..." God made man healthy and wealthy, so who made man prone to sickness and lack?

> *"...from the beginning it was not so" Matthew 19:8*

Child of God, you are not the sick seeking for healing, you are the healthy who satan has made sick. You are not the poor seeking to be rich but the wealthy one who satan is trying to make poor. You are not the barren seeking to be fruitful; you are the fruitful who satan is trying to deny their fruitfulness.

You were neither created with any sickness; nor were you created poor. You were neither created a servant to your mates nor were you created a slave to your younger ones. So why is your life the way it is?

Matt. 13:24-28 records Jesus' famous parable of the wheat and the tares. It talks about a man who planted good seeds in his field, but while men slept, the enemy came and planted tares, and went his way. Both seeds began to grow and when the servants of the owner of the field noticed this, they asked him how the tares came about. His response was "an enemy has done this".

> *And Joshua called for them, and he spake unto them, saying, Wherefore have ye beguiled us, saying, We are very far from you; when ye dwell among us? Now therefore ye are cursed, and there shall none of you be freed from being bondmen, and hewers of wood and drawers of water for the house of my God And Joshua made them that day hewers of wood and drawers of*

> *water for the congregation, and for the altar of the LORD, even unto this day, in the place which he should choose. Joshua 9: 22-23 & 27*

In the passage above, the Gibeonites deceived Joshua and the elders of Israel into establishing a covenant with them by pretending that they came from a far country. Three days later, when Joshua got to know that they had deceived him, he was understandably upset and the scripture records that he proceeded to make them that day, hewers of wood and drawers of water. The emphasis is that, HE MADE THEM.

He made some pronouncements, and their destiny as a people was altered. He made them to serve the children of Israel where he chose. These men were educated, intelligent and rich. They were so clever that they could come up with the idea, and actually alter the chemical composition of their clothes so well that the elders were all deceived. However, in one day, by the pronouncement of one aggrieved man, all of their potentials, wisdom and education was rubbished and they became slaves.

Countless people are struggling in life because of a "Joshua" who has tampered with their originality. It wasn't God, but a man who made the Gibeonites slaves by the words of his mouth. This goes to show that some of man's sufferings are man-made or man -

inflicted. There are people who have power in their tongue to affect people's destinies. Jezebel spoke and charismatic prophet Elijah folded up his ministry. Joseph's brothers spoke and he, the favourite child ended up as a slave. Pharaoh spoke and the favoured Hebrews were turned to slaves. Herod spoke and vibrant John the Baptist lost his life. Delilah spoke and mighty Samson lost his anointing and ministry.

Drop this book in your hands right now and pray this prayer with holy anger; ***Oh Lord, every manifestation of the hand of man contrary to Your perfect will for my life, let it wither now by fire, in the name of Jesus!***

"*Joshua made them that day...*" Their misery began in one day. Whatever misery that may be in your life now, started one day when the "Joshua" against your destiny spoke certain words and your destiny turned upside down. As God's servant, I speak into your life today, and I command an immediate reversal of whatever was spoken or done against you, in the name of Jesus. Amen!

I declare and decree over every one reading this book:

* **That day programmed to alter your divine destiny will not come!**
* **That day programmed to close your marital destiny will not come!**
* **That day programmed to rubbish your financial destiny will not come!**
* **That day programmed to change your**

business destiny will not come!

* **That day programmed to destroy your health will not come!**
* **That day programmed to close your womb will not come, in the mighty name of Jesus!**
* **I cancel the day of tragedy programmed against your life.**
* **I cancel the day of untimely death programmed against your life.**
* **I cancel the day of failure programmed against you.**
* **Any accident programmed against your life is cancelled.**
* **I cancel the day of mysterious exchange against your destiny.**
* **That day programmed to alter your academic destiny will not come, in the mighty name of Jesus. Amen!**

When you are made to serve an altar, the altar dictates the direction of your life. Joshua knew the power of the altar, hence he made the Gibeonites slaves of the altar. This is the picture of many today, who have been sold to the altars in their families by the strong man.

The altar is the power that enforced Joshua's utterance and that is why even after his death, the Gibeonites remained slaves because the altar continued to carry out the instructions of Joshua.

We find a similar occurrence in the book of Joshua 6:26 where Joshua laid a curse on whosoever would rise up in the future to rebuild the wall of Jericho. Several years later in 1st Kings 16:34, his words came to pass even though Joshua by then, was long dead.

> *And Joshua adjured them at that time, saying, Cursed be the man before the LORD, that riseth up and buildeth this city Jericho: he shall lay the foundation thereof in his firstborn, and in his youngest son shall he set up the gates of it. Joshua 6:26*
>
> *In his days did Hiel the Bethelite build Jericho: he laid the foundation thereof in Abiram his firstborn, and set up the gates thereof in his youngest son Segub, according to the word of the LORD, which he spake by Joshua the son of Nun. 1Kings 16:34*

* Today, I decree a new and better law into existence in your life!
* Your prosperity shall have no limit!
* Your body shall accommodate no sickness!
* Your enemies shall come out against you in one way but they shall scatter in seven ways!

* Opportunities shall pursue and overtake you!
* I decree unusual favour into your life!
* Health and wealth shall be your garment!
* I decree intelligence and outstanding wisdom on your children!
* I decree success in the place where you failed before!
* I decree an end to all afflictions in your life!
* I decree an end to a life of hardship and struggles for you!
* I decree an end to every form of barrenness, miscarriage and still-birth in your life!
* I decree financial overflow, in the mighty name of Jesus!

The mad man of Gadara in Mark 5:1-8, was not created with madness. Like everyone else created by God, he was destined to be great and live amongst normal people; but that was not his reality, he lived in the graveyard for several years until he met Jesus. The question is, who made him like that?

Everyone speaking evil into your life is hereby condemned today, in the mighty name of Jesus.

> *Let not an evil speaker be established in the earth: evil shall hunt the violent man to overthrow him. Psalm 140:11*

WHEN "JOSHUA" SPEAKS, THE FOLLOWING HAPPENS

DISPLACEMENT

The mad man was made to live where he was not created to live. There are people like this who have been displaced in life, they live where they are not supposed to live, work where they are not supposed to work and generally live a life that isn't theirs. Examine your life, is this where you should be in life with all your gifts, qualifications and/or experience? With all the people you know, is this the level you should be at? With your beauty and good family upbringing should you still remain single at this age? A "Joshua" has kept you where you are to prevent you from getting to where you ought to be.

LACK OF HELPERS

No man could tame the mad man of Gadara. No one could help him. When the strong man has tampered with your destiny, they make it impossible for people to help you by driving away your helpers.
They make sure they render you helpless, directly or indirectly. In Matthew 27:60-65, the king instructed the soldiers to ensure that Jesus doesn't come out, so they rolled a big stone over the door of the grave and put the seal of the king on it so that any man who had a mind to bring Him out would be discouraged when they see the king's seal. Even if He awakens from

death and cries out for help to come out from the tomb, nobody would come to His help because of the king's seal on the great stone.

If your own experience is a dearth of helpers, may divine helpers locate you now, in Jesus' name.

CONTINUOS SUFFERING

The life of the mad man made him weep continuously, day and night. This is the reality of some people; if they don't cry in January, they will cry in March, if they don't cry in the morning, they cry in the evening, some even cry in the midnight! Their joy is characteristically short lived. Nothing good lasts with them because there will always be issues that make them cry. Any yoke of perpetual suffering in your life, is broken today, in the name of Jesus!

ADDICTION

He was cutting himself with stones and bleeding, yet he could not stop it. Some people are like that - they are doing things which cause them harm, yet they can't stop it. They are destroying themselves through addiction to hard drugs, fornication, adultery, prostitution, pornography, masturbation, drunkenness, crime, etc. The devil knows that evil patterns are enforced and recycled by evil habits so he ensures that his victims are entrenched in destructive habits so they can remain slaves to the evil patterns.

A LIFE OF SLAVERY

When "Joshua" speaks against you, you find yourself serving others against your will. Irrespective of your field of endeavor, your potentials, knowledge and wisdom are used to benefit others yet you are paid a pittance. Even if such a person studies "Extra-Terrestrial Engineering", they will still serve others and remain poor. Slaves do not negotiate their wages and they always work harder than they are remunerated. Slavery is generational except someone revolts and stops it by force. Freedom is never given willingly by the oppressor; it must be demanded for and taken by force. That is why you notice many poor people had poor parents and if they don't do anything about it, their own children will continue the journey in poverty.

EIGHT

MYSTERIES OF ANCESTRAL PENALTY

Chapter Eight

"

*Ancestral penalty is
the manifestation of a curse
on the present generation for
sins committed by their ancestors.*

"

Chapter Eight

MYSTERIES OF ANCESTRAL PENALTY

•●⬤●•

Remember, O LORD, what is come upon us: consider, and behold our reproach. Our inheritance is turned to strangers, our houses to aliens. We are orphans and fatherless, our mothers are as widows. We have drunken our water for money; our wood is sold unto us. Our necks are under persecution: we labour, and have no rest. We have given the hand to the Egyptians, and to the Assyrians, to be satisfied with bread. OUR FATHERS HAVE SINNED, AND ARE NOT; AND WE HAVE BORNE THEIR INIQUITIES. LAM. 5:1-7

Ancestral penalty is the punishment established by law for crime or offence committed by your ancestors. It is suffering or punishment for the sin of others simply because they are your progenitors. It is official punishment and payback for the evil deeds of your parents.

Ancestral penalty is the manifestation of a curse on present generation for sins committed by their ancestors. It is spiritual sanctions imposed on your life because of what your ancestors got involved in. It is repercussion for the evil deeds of your ancestors.

Ancestral penalty is paying for what you did not buy. It is atoning for the wickedness of past generations. It is the consequence of a cursed family tree and suffering because of wrong family foundation. This is a very serious issue because it means forfeiting your destiny due to the errors of your ancestors.

Many persons are suffering the consequences of generational curses and calamity from past generations to the present. Ancestral penalty can stop you on the way to greatness because of your lineage. It can sentence you to untimely death if your DNA carries the death penalty. It manifests in untold hardships, pains, losses, defeat, delays, stagnation, poverty, sicknesses and ultimately, untimely death.

> *Then there was a famine in the days of David three years, year*

after year; and David enquired of the LORD. And the LORD answered, It is for Saul, and for his bloody house, because he slew the Gibeonites. And the king called the Gibeonites, and said unto them; (now the Gibeonites were not of the children of Israel, but of the remnant of the Amorites; and the children of Israel had sworn unto them: and Saul sought to slay them in his zeal to the children of Israel and Judah.) Wherefore David said unto the Gibeonites, What shall I do for you? and wherewith shall I make the atonement, that ye may bless the inheritance of the LORD? And the Gibeonites said unto him, We will have no silver nor gold of Saul, nor of his house; neither for us shalt thou kill any man in Israel. And he said, What ye shall say, that will I do for you. And they answered the king, The man that consumed us, and that devised against us that we should be destroyed from remaining in any of the coasts of Israel, Let seven men of his sons be delivered unto us, and we will hang them up unto the LORD in Gibeah of Saul, whom the LORD did choose. And the king said, I will give them. But the king spared MEPHIBOSHETH, the son of Jonathan the son of Saul, because of the LORD'S oath that was between them, between David and Jonathan the son of Saul. But the king took the two sons of Rizpah the daughter of Aiah, whom she bare unto Saul, Armoni and MEPHIBOSHETH; and the five sons of Michal the daughter of Saul, whom she brought up for Adriel the son of Barzillai the Meholathite: And he delivered them into the hands of the Gibeonites, and they hanged them in the hill before the LORD: and they fell all seven together, and were put to death in the days of harvest, in the first days, in the beginning of barley harvest. And the bones of Saul and Jonathan his son buried they in the country of Benjamin in Zelah, in the sepulchre of Kish his father: and they performed all that the king commanded. AND AFTER

T H A T G O D W A S INTREATED FOR THE LAND.

David and the entire nation of Israel suffered three years of famine because of the sin of Saul, who broke the covenant which Joshua entered into with the Gibeonites in Joshua 9:1-20. David did not know the reason for the calamity which befell the land until he asked God, who then revealed that he was paying the penalty for Saul's wickedness against the Gibeonites. To stop the famine, two sons of Saul and five sons of Michal, Saul's daughter that she bore to Adriel, were sacrificed at the prime of their lives for sins they did not commit. T*he beginning of harvest speaks of* the time when their lives were about to flourish and make impact in their generation; that was when they were cut short.

One shocking thing I noticed here was that Mephibosheth, the son of Jonathan, who was also a descendant of Saul, was spared, and the reason was because of the covenant that existed between David and his late father, Jonathan. In the same family where some died because an ancient covenant was broken, one person escaped because an ancient covenant was honoured.

In fact, there was a Mephiboseth, the son of Rizpah who was not spared from the onslaught, but another Mephiboseth was spared because another covenant was speaking for him. They were cousins and bare the same name, yet they had a different experience. If you like, change your name to Goodluck, if an old covenant militating against you remains unbroken, your life might even become worse after you effect the change of name!

Jabez did not change his name but he entreated the God of Heaven and his situation was reversed. He knew that merely changing his name by himself would amount to chasing a shadow - an exercise in futility.

POSTPONEMENT OF CALAMITY

Behold, I will bring evil upon thee, and will take away thy posterity, and will cut off from Ahab him that pisseth against the wall, and him that is shut up and left in Israel, And will make thine house like the house of Jeroboam the son of Nebat, and like the house of Baasha the son of Ahijah, for the provocation wherewith thou hast provoked me to anger, and made Israel to sin. And of Jezebel also spake the LORD, saying, The dogs shall eat Jezebel by the wall of Jezreel. Him that dieth of Ahab in the city the dogs shall eat; and him that dieth in the field shall the fowls of the air eat. But there was none like unto Ahab, which did sell himself to work wickedness in the sight of the LORD, whom Jezebel his wife stirred up. And he did very abominably in following idols, according to all things as did the Amorites, whom the LORD cast out before the children of Israel. And it came to pass, when Ahab heard those words, that he rent his clothes, and put sackcloth upon his flesh, and fasted, and lay in sackcloth, and went softly. And the word of the LORD came to Elijah the Tishbite, saying, Seest thou how Ahab humbleth himself before me? because he humbleth himself before me, I will not bring the evil in his days: but in his son's days will I bring the evil upon his house. 1st KINGS. 21:21-29

Ahab committed many evil deeds including the killing of Naboth and seizing of his father's inheritance. This made God angry and He pronounced curses on him. He said He would *take away his posterity,* destroy his male children and visit his family with strange death so that their corpses will not be buried, but rather eaten by beasts.

I don't know who counseled Ahab, but when he heard these ominous pronouncements, he repented in his heart and entered into compulsory fasting. By this repentant attitude, he succeeded in averting the evil in his days and it was postponed to the time of his children.

> *And it came to pass, when Joram saw Jehu, that he said, Is it peace, Jehu? And he answered, What peace, so long as the whoredoms of thy mother Jezebel and her witchcrafts are so many? And Joram turned his hands, and fled, and said to Ahaziah, There is treachery, O Ahaziah. And Jehu drew a bow with his full strength, and smote Jehoram between his arms, and the arrow went out at his heart, and he sunk down in his chariot. Then said Jehu to Bidkar his captain, Take up, and cast him in the portion of the field of Naboth the Jezreelite: for remember how that, when I and thou rode together after Ahab his father, the LORD laid this burden upon him; 2Kings 9:22-25*

Joram, Ahab's son, paid with his life for the sins of his father and was not buried. Also, in 2 Kings 10:6-7, seventy innocent sons of Ahab paid the penalty and died a cheap death, even those who were associated with them became victims also.

> *Then he wrote a letter the second time to them, saying, If ye be mine, and if ye will hearken unto my voice, take ye the heads of the men your master's sons, and come to me to Jezreel by tomorrow this time. Now the king's sons, being seventy persons, were with the great men of the city, which brought them up. And it came to pass, when the letter came to them, that they took the king's sons, and slew seventy persons, and put their heads in baskets, and sent him them to Jezreel.*

LOSS OF PRIESTLY INHERITANCE.

Prophet Eli's inability to correct the wickedness of his children attracted curses on his family. Years later, a generation that did not know what happened paid the price for his mistakes.

> *Behold, the days come, that I will*

cut off thine arm, and the arm of thy father's house, that THERE SHALL NOT BE AN OLD MAN IN THINE HOUSE. And thou shalt see an enemy in my habitation, in all the wealth which God shall give Israel: and THERE SHALL NOT BE AN OLD MAN IN THINE HOUSE FOR EVER. And the man of thine, whom I shall not cut off from mine altar, shall be to consume thine eyes, and to grieve thine heart: and ALL THE INCREASE OF THINE HOUSE SHALL DIE IN THE FLOWER OF THEIR AGE. And this shall be a sign unto thee, that shall come upon thy two sons, on Hophni and Phinehas; in one day they shall die both of them. And I will raise me up a faithful priest that shall do according to that which is in mine heart and in my mind: and I will build him a sure house; and he shall walk before mine anointed forever. And it shall come to pass, that every one that is left in thine house shall come and crouch to him for a piece of

> *silver and a morsel of bread, and shall say, Put me, I pray thee, into one of the priests' offices, that I may eat a piece of bread. 1 SAM 2:31-36*

Eli not only lost his priesthood but also disenfranchised his entire lineage from serving God in that capacity. He delivered his generation into untimely death even before they were born. He smeared the wealth of his future generations with poverty. What a terrible thing to pass onto the next generation!

GENERATIONAL SICKNESS

After the death of king Saul, Abner, the influential captain of his army, thought it wise to make peace with David. On his way from the reconciliatory meeting, Joab, the captain of David's army met and killed him in retaliation for a wrong done him in a previous war. David was very displeased with Joab and pronounced specific curses on him and his family to the effect that: (a) there would always be a leper in Joab's family (b) there would always be paralytic fellows in his family, (c) they would always experience tragic and violent death, (d) poverty would not depart from his lineage forever! (1Sam. 2&3)

Also in 2kings 5:27, Elisha pronounced leprosy on

Gehazi and his seed forever. A careful look through the Bible will show you various curses and their effects upon the real or perceived offender; unfortunately, the effects of these curses usually spill over to innocent people who are connected to the original victims of the curse.

LOSS OF KINGDOM INHERITANCE

In 1 Kings 11:6,11-12, the sins of Solomon brought curses on his innocent son Rehoboam, and denied him his inheritance. Rehoboam was qualified to inherit the twelve tribes of Israel from his father just as his father had inherited from his own father, David. But Solomon's sin of idol worship transferred ten of the tribes to his servant, leaving Rehoboam the rightful king, with only two tribes!

REPROACH IN THE LAND OF PLENTY

> *And the LORD said unto Joshua, This day have I rolled away the reproach of Egypt from off you. Wherefore the name of the place is called Gilgal unto this day. Josh. 5:9*

The children of Israel entered the land flowing with milk and honey, yet they were still eating only manna because of the reproach of Egypt where their parents came from. They were in the midst of plenty, in the presence of their promised possession but they could not feed of the fat of the land because of the reproach that was on their parents. Although they did not know Egypt, the reproach of Egypt was in their DNA and until they did the needful as commanded by God, the reproach was not rolled away.

EFFECTS OF CURSES

1. Unexplainable denial of the good things of life in spite of tireless efforts.
2. Loss of what one has acquired in order to keep him from attaining a new level.
3. Constant failure in life endeavours.
4. Untimely death in the family.
5. Strange hereditary sickness in the family.
6. Poverty.
7. Tragic and violent death.
8. Limitations in all areas or a particular direction that will enhance one's life.
9. Confusion and ceaseless quarrels in the family.
10. Barrenness or miscarriage.

NINE

COVENANT WEAPONS FOR BINDING THE STRONGMAN

Chapter Nine

"

For you to have total victory, you must first have faith that God will deliver you and that your prayers will be answered.

"

Chapter Nine

COVENANT WEAPONS FOR BINDING THE STRONGMAN

•●⬤●•

> *For the WEAPONS of our warfare are not carnal, but MIGHTY through God to the pulling down of strong holds.* **2 Cor. 10:4**

> *For we wrestle not against flesh and blood, but against principalities, against powers, against the rulers of the darkness of this world, against spiritual wickedness in high places.* **Eph. 6:12**

In the above scriptures, Apostle Paul made us understand that to engage the war in the spirit and conquer the strong man, you must be equipped with powerful weapons of God.

The weapons must be mighty because the strong man is what he is - a *"strong man"*. God has given us mighty weapons with which to conquer him; but we must know how to put them to use appropriately *because a weapon you don't know how to use is not only useless to you, but also very dangerous because it can cause you harm.*

Weapon #1

AGGRESSIVE PRAYERS IN THE NAME OF JESUS

The prayer of binding and loosing in the name of Jesus, is one of the weapons that the Lord has given us. The strong man can only be disarmed when a *stronger than he* comes and the strongest name in all realms is the name of Jesus!

> *When a strong man armed keepeth his palace, his goods are in peace: But when a stronger than he shall come upon him, and overcome him, he taketh from him all his armour wherein he trusted, and divideth his spoils.* **Luke 11:21 -22**

> *Wherefore God also hath highly exalted him, and given him a name which is above every name:*

> *That at the name of Jesus every knee should bow, of things in heaven, and things in earth, and things under the earth;* **Phil. 2:9-10**

No matter how strong the strong man is, God is still the King of the universe, and without controversy, His power far surpasses every other power. One of the greatest avenues through which God displays His strength is through a church or believer that prevails in prayers.

> *Verily I say unto you, Whatsoever ye shall bind on earth shall be bound in heaven: and whatsoever ye shall loose on earth shall be loosed in heaven. Mat 18:18*

If satan has been able to set up his throne and dominion in your life and family, it's because you have not yet overpowered the strong man in aggressive *intercession.*

I am not talking about weak, repetitive prayers that cannot move even a pebble; I am talking of persistent aggressive prayers released from a *heart of faith. It is this* that can move mountains.

However, if you embark on these prayers without

faith in your heart, you are only carrying out an exercise in futility. **For you to have total victory, you must first have faith that God will deliver you and that your prayers will be answered. (Heb.11:6)**

It doesn't matter how long the strong man has been ruling in your family, or how long you have been held bound by the satanic strong man sent against your life, the strong man is still a "man" and since that is the case, then he is subject to your God. Alleluia!

> *Is any among you afflicted? Let him pray. James 5:13a*
>
> *...The effectual fervent prayer of a righteous man availeth much. James 5:16b*

A fascinating instance of how intercessors in one nation conquered their strongman is a testimony from Panama. Different Panamanians have described the agony of their years under the harsh dictatorship of Manuel Noriega. They shared about the sound of helicopters in the night that flew over the jungles and dropped black garbage bags containing the remains of those who posed real or imaginary threats to his dictatorship. It was a well-known fact that Noriega consorted with occult leaders and practiced voodoo and other forms of magic. The empowerment he received from these dark forces protected him for a season and during that period he seemed indeed to be an invincible strong man.

However, various Christian leaders in the country organized a united prayer army. This army understood that the weapons of their warfare were not carnal, but mighty through God for pulling down strongholds and strong men! They harnessed their spiritual weapons through prayer in a unique way—all-night prayers by bus! The intercessors would pray throughout the whole nation once a month in this manner: while a leader led the prayers through radio broadcast, those interceding in the buses agreed together with those who had to stay at home with their families. The strong man's troops never suspected they were being spiritually overthrown in such a "harmless" manner. Most of you know the end of the story—prayer always works! Noriega was deposed and sent to prison in the United States!

If organized prayer can remove a national strong man, why do you think if you organize yourself to pray fervently, you can't unseat the strong man in your life or family?

If, as you begin to pray, you notice some sort of resistance or counter attack, don't stop the prayers, rather reinforce it by:

1. *Declaring a fast.*
2. *Invoking the Blood of Jesus.*
3. *Prompt obedience to divine instructions.*

4. *Taking a painful (sacrificial) seed to your man of God.*
5. *Engaging in prophetic praise and worship sessions.*

When you do these, you have succeeded in taking the *battle to a higher plane.* The unpleasant reaction you might observe or experience when you begin the prayers is a ploy from the pit of hell to distract or force you to stop because your prayer is already creating problems for them. There is a realm your prayers get to that even the strongest of strong men will be demobilized and rendered powerless.

Sometime ago, venomous snakes were being shipped from Africa to Europe in a plane. Unfortunately, the person who packed the snakes forgot to lock the box in which the snakes were placed. As soon as the plane took off, the snakes began to respond to the movement of the plane and found their way out of the box.

Passengers in the plane could see various snakes on the isle. They screamed, some fainted and the brave ones took refuge wherever they could within the plane.

The air-hostess ran to the pilot to inform him of this scary development and he quickly informed the Air Traffic Controller on the ground. Here's an excerpt of the conversation that took place between them:

Pilot: "We are extremely sorry. The passenger who got these snakes had forgotten to lock the box. These are poisonous snakes, so where can I land? Please advise me before passengers get bitten."

Air Traffic Controller: "No, do not land. Stay there for a minute, let me think."

Surely this sounded like a bit of stupid advice to the desperate pilot- a minute was too long in the face of such danger, but he had to follow the orders of the Air Traffic Controller. After a minute, the Air Traffic Controller got back to the distressed pilot.

Air Traffic Controller: "At what altitude are you flying?"
Pilot: "300"
Air Traffic Controller: "Go higher"
Pilot: "But the snakes will …"
Air Traffic Controller: "I said, go higher!" (Moments later, he asked again) "Now, what's your altitude?"
Pilot: "500.67"
Air Traffic Controller: "Go higher"
Pilot: "But Sir..."
Air Traffic Controller: "I said, go higher, Captain."

(The Pilot complied. By now, the snakes were all over the plane and tension had mounted. A few passengers had been bitten and were now unconscious. The other passengers were still scrambling, seeking refuge anywhere in the plane).

Air Traffic Controller: "Now Captain, keep on going higher."
(The Pilot complied and kept on going higher and higher).
Air Traffic Controller: "Now what's your altitude?"
Pilot: "Now I am on 1200"
Air Traffic Controller: "Now stay there. Tell the cabin crew that at this altitude, the snakes are now harmless. They can just pick them up with their hands and return them to the box, and this time they should not forget to lock it."

One cabin crew tried holding a snake. It was numb and harmless. Soon it became a game among passengers in the plane. For the first time, some were holding snakes in their hands and returning them to the box.

"Look at this black Mamba, it was really after me. Now I can even throw it and catch it like a ball", said one passenger.

This was how a life threatening situation in the plane was turned around and it became fun. Those who had fainted were quickly resuscitated and no life was lost.

Fact: Snakes, at high altitude usually stop moving and eventually die!

The moral here is that there is need for you to increase

the altitude of your prayer life. Surely, there is a point you reach in your prayers and you just know that at this point, even the most seemingly unconquerable problems get defeated and the strongman loses every power over you!

Herod began breathing fire down the necks of the Apostles and he stretched forth his hand and killed James. Perhaps the church carried placards and marched round the city in protest but it only made Herod more blood thirsty. Since the church said nothing to God, God did nothing for the church. But when he stretched his hands and took Peter, the church abandoned physical strategies and took the battle to a realm higher than Herod. The Bible says prayer was made! That means prayer was "produced", being "churned out" non- stop!

> *Now about that time Herod the king stretched forth his hands to vex certain of the church. And he killed James the brother of John with the sword. And because he saw it pleased the Jews, he proceeded further to take Peter also. (Then were the days of unleavened bread.) And when he had apprehended him, he put him in prison, and delivered him to four quaternions of soldiers to keep him; intending after Easter*

to bring him forth to the people.
Peter therefore was kept in
prison: BUT PRAYER WAS
MADE WITHOUT CEASING
of the church unto God for him.
Acts 12:1-5

Oh! How wonderful and glorious your life will be if you can catch and appropriate this revelation to your life. They did not pray prayer, they MADE prayer! They prayed to the extent that God had to send an angel from heaven to effect a dramatic escape for Peter!

And when Herod would have brought him forth, the same night Peter was sleeping between two soldiers, bound with two chains: and the keepers before the door kept the prison. And, behold, the angel of the Lord came upon him, and a light shined in the prison: and he smote Peter on the side, and raised him up, saying, Arise up quickly. And his chains fell off from his hands. And the angel said unto him, Gird thyself, and bind on thy sandals. And so he did. And he saith unto him, Cast thy garment about thee, and follow me. And he went out, and

> *followed him; and wist not that it was true which was done by the angel; but thought he saw a vision. When they were past the first and the second ward, they came unto the iron gate that leadeth unto the city; which opened to them of his own accord: and they went out, and passed on through one street; and forthwith the angel departed from him. Acts 12:6-10*

The deliverance was so supernatural that even Apostle Peter doubted it was happening in real life, he thought rather, that he was in a vision. These people vowed that they would not stop praying until they saw the results of their prayers. They decided that they would not hold their peace until God intervened.

> *I have set watchmen upon thy walls, O Jerusalem, which shall never hold their peace day nor night: ye that make mention of the LORD, KEEP NOT SILENCE, AND GIVE HIM NO REST, till he establish, and till he make Jerusalem a praise in the earth. Isa 62:6-7*

They prayed to the extent that the only thing that could interrupt their prayer was the answer! Dear reader, ***I prophesy into your life this day, as you embark on aggressive prayers, you will be interrupted only by answers from Heaven, in the name of Jesus!***

> *And when Peter was come to himself, he said, Now I know of a surety, that the Lord hath sent his angel, and hath delivered me out of the hand of Herod, and from all the expectation of the people of the Jews. And when he had considered the thing, he came to the house of Mary the mother of John, whose surname was Mark; WHERE MANY WERE GATHERED TOGETHER PRAYING. And as Peter knocked at the door of the gate, a damsel came to hearken, named Rhoda. And when she knew Peter's voice, she opened not the gate for gladness, but ran in, and told how Peter stood before the gate. And they said unto her, Thou art mad. But she constantly affirmed that it was even so. Then said they, It is his angel. But Peter continued*

> *knocking: and when they had opened the door, and saw him, they were astonished. Acts 12:11-16*

They did not stop there, they knew that the deliverance of Peter was not enough to deter Herod except he (Herod) was terminated. The Bible says in Psalms 7:9 "*Oh let the wickedness of the wicked come to an end; but establish the just: for the righteous God trieth the hearts and reins.*" The only way the wickedness of the wicked can truly come to an end is if the wicked repents or if the wicked himself comes to an end. The early church continued in protracted and violent prayers until God smote Herod and he died a shameful and fearful death. Then, *the Word of God grew and multiplied! Alleluia!*

> *And when Herod had sought for him, and found him not, he examined the keepers, and commanded that they should be put to death. And he went down from Judaea to Caesarea, and there abode. And Herod was highly displeased with them of Tyre and Sidon: but they came with one accord to him, and, having made Blastus the king's chamberlain their friend, desired peace; because their country was*

> *nourished by the king's country. And upon a set day Herod, arrayed in royal apparel, sat upon his throne, and made an oration unto them. And the people gave a shout, saying, It is the voice of a god, and not of a man. And immediately the angel of the Lord smote him, because he gave not God the glory: and he was eaten of worms, and gave up the ghost. BUT THE WORD OF GOD GREW AND MULTIPLIED.* Acts 12:19-24

You have tremendous power in the place of prayer; use it to depose of that strong man and secure your freedom.

Queen Mary of Scotland said concerning John Knox, who was a man of prayer, "I fear the prayers of John Knox more than all the assembled armies of Europe."

> *Confess your faults one to another, and pray one for another, that ye may be healed. THE EFFECTUAL FERVENT PRAYER OF A RIGHTEOUS MAN AVAILETH MUCH. James 5:16*

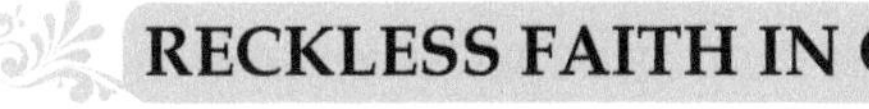

RECKLESS FAITH IN GOD

Whenever I read or hear the story of David and Goliath, I do not cease to wonder at David's guts and whatever it was that gave him the boldness and confidence to embark on what seemed like a suicide mission. From all physical indications, David was no match for even the armour bearer of Goliath, not to talk of Goliath himself. He was not a warrior neither was he a trained soldier. He had no business in the battle field and I want to believe that was the first battle scene David was witnessing. The entire army of Israel including Saul the king, had been overcome by fear at the mere sight of Goliath, because of his antecedent as the champion from Gath.

> *And all the men of Israel, when they saw the man, fled from him, and were sore afraid. 1Sam 17:24*

David didn't care about any of that, all that mattered to him was that this opponent was an uncircumcised Philistine and he had defied the armies of the most High God, his God.

Child of God, this strong man may have succeeded in destroying the lives of others before you. He may have even succeeded in your life before now, but not anymore.

To conquer a force that appears stronger than you requires reckless faith in God. When your faith is in God, it will show in the way you address the strongman. When you put your faith in God, you tactically remove yourself from the fight like David did and pitch your enemy against your God.

> *And David spake to the men that stood by him, saying, WHAT SHALL BE DONE TO THE MAN THAT KILLETH THIS PHILISTINE, and taketh away the reproach from Israel? For who is this uncircumcised Philistine, that he should defy the armies of the living God? 1Sam 17:26*

David did not ask; "what shall be done to the person who **attempts** to fight this powerful giant?" Instead he asked, "What shall be done to the man who **kills** this Philistine?" In David's mind, Goliath was already dead. If he did not have faith in God's ability to kill Goliath, he would not have been bold enough to negotiate or ask about his reward even before the fight.

FAITH IS PROVOKED BY PREVIOUS TESTIMONIES OF GOD'S DELIVERANCE

> *And they overcame him by the blood of the Lamb, and by the*

word of their TESTIMONY;
and they loved not their lives
unto the death. Rev 12:11

If you look back in the journey of your life, you will recall numerous times when God delivered you from situations where you had concluded that all hope was lost. Recalling such situations helps to boost your faith as you believe Him to deliver you again in this present challenge.

And Saul said to David, Thou art not able to go against this Philistine to fight with him: for thou art but a youth, and he a man of war from his youth. And David said unto Saul, Thy servant kept his father's sheep, and there came a lion, and a bear, and took a lamb out of the flock: And I went out after him, and smote him, and delivered it out of his mouth: and when he arose against me, I caught him by his beard, and smote him, and slew him. Thy servant slew both the lion and the bear: and this uncircumcised Philistine shall be as one of them, seeing he hath defied the armies of the living God. David said moreover, THE LORD THAT

> *DELIVERED ME OUT OF THE PAW OF THE LION, AND OUT OF THE PAW OF THE BEAR, HE WILL DELIVER ME OUT OF THE HAND OF THIS PHILISTINE. And Saul said unto David, Go, and the LORD be with thee. 1Sam 17:33-37*

FAITH IS PROVOKED BY THE WORD OF GOD

> *So then faith cometh by hearing, and hearing by the word of God. Rom. 10:17*

A Wordless believer is a faithless believer. The world we live in is governed by laws, decrees and legislations. *We understand by faith that the world was designed by the Word of God.* Now if the world was framed by the Word of God, it means that the world can also be reframed by the same Word of God.

> *Through faith we understand that the worlds were framed by the word of God, so that things which are seen were not made of things which do appear. Heb. 11:3*

Knowledge of the Word strengthens you and

enforces your prayer for speedy answers. In fact, knowledge of the Word gives you double assurance when you make demands in faith. If you don't know what is obtainable by His Word, how can you make intelligent legislation in the courts of Heaven?

THE MYSTERY OF SACRIFICE

This is one *secret* that is so open yet it's still hidden from many believers because our human nature is basically selfish. Unfortunately, the children of darkness seem to have gained deeper insight into the mystery of sacrifice, and they employ it in negative ways. Satan invented nothing; all that the kingdom of darkness has are perverted principles and practices from God's sacred Word.

A sacrifice is an action carried out by mortals to create a vacuum for God to fill. It is a painful experience that gives a gainful result. **It is the value you have for your dream, destiny, vision and goal that drives you to make the needed sacrifices to achieve them.** God placed premium value on us hence He offered His only begotten Son as sacrifice for our redemption. No one succeeds in life without making needed sacrifices for that success and no business succeeds without sacrifice. Likewise, no marriage, ministry or any venture for that matter succeeds without necessary sacrifices.

Do you value total deliverance from the strong man

that is after your life? Are you willing to give up something you love, a kind of life you cherish in order to provoke your freedom?

1. Joseph sacrificed for about thirteen years to enter early satisfaction at the age of thirty.
2. David sacrificed for about thirteen years to enter the throne at age thirty.
3. Esther sacrificed in intense prayers combined with dry fasting and to prepare a banquet for the king and changed the evil decree of Haman in order to save her people. (Esther chapters 5 & 6)
4. Solomon sacrificed so much on God's altar to attract God's attention and he got an uncommon answer. (1 Kings. 3:4-14)
5. Gideon came out of poverty and became a Judge in Israel by sacrifice. (Judges 6:25-33)

Sacrifice on God's altar is a mystery to end miseries in life. It provokes quick response from God and terminates delay. It did for Hannah, and it will do same for you because Jesus Christ is the same yesterday, today and forever!

By one painful sacrifice of His precious Son Jesus, God legitimately conquered and redeemed the earth from the grips of satan forever. *(John 3:16.)*

It took a daring and urgent sacrifice from David at the threshing floor of Araunah to stay the hand of the angel of death sent to destroy Israel. (*2 Sam 24:15-25).*

By that singular sacrifice, David ended the plague that had already killed seventy thousand men in three days. Sacrifice will end prolonged and protracted challenges in your life.

The King of Moab was engaged in a battle with God's chosen nation, Israel. It is important to note that Israel had gone into this battle with God's assurance of victory. As the battle increased, the king of Moab mustered his most valiant soldiers, yet they could not prevail. When he ran out of ideas and strategies and utter defeat loomed before him, this heathen king, knew better and quickly applied this strategy - he took hold of his first son who would have reigned after him, and offered him as a sacrifice! The Bible records that after he did this, there was great indignation against the children of Israel and they returned from pursuing him (2 Kings 3:4-27). Do you wonder why God would cause events to turn out like this in this battle? I believe that the vital lesson God wants His children to learn in this story is the undisputable power of a painful sacrifice in reversing an evil trend or terminating an unfavourable course. He is a God of principles and whosoever applies the principles, gets the accompanying result!

Sacrifice is that one stone in your hand that kills the Goliath of your life. By sacrifice, four hundred and thirty years of slavery which the enemy had wanted to continue forever was dramatically terminated. (Exodus 13) By sacrifice, Abraham obtained the transgenerational covenant of wealth. (Gen. 22:1-18)

Whatever you sacrifice yourself for will in turn sacrifice itself for you. You need to make that sacrifice to secure your total deliverance and to provoke the manifestation of your dominion in your generation. Take advantage of the time you are in and make that sacrifice for the changes you desire. Act now!

For more in-depth study of the Mystery of Sacrifice in negotiating your freedom, see my book; *Mysteries of the Altars*

As you engage these weapons holistically, I see God facilitating your healing, restoration, promotion and total deliverance, I see Him doing for you what no one else could have ever done.

TEN

FIFTY (50) VIOLENT PRAYER POINTS FOR BINDING THE STRONG MAN

Chapter Ten

"And from the days of John the Baptist until now, the kingdom of heaven suffereth violence, and the violent taketh it by force." Matthew 11:12

Chapter Ten

FIFTY (50) VIOLENT PRAYER POINTS FOR BINDING THE STRONGMAN

•●⬤●•

"And from the days of John the Baptist until now, the kingdom of heaven suffereth violence, and the violent taketh it by force." Matthew 11:12

1. I cover myself with the blood of Jesus as I bind the strong man holding me captive, in the mighty name of Jesus.
2. Heavenly Father, I thank You for Your assurance of consistent victory in every battle, in the name of Jesus.
3. You occultic strong man of my father's house, hear my voice; I arrest you now, in the mighty name of Jesus.
4. You satanic strong man fighting God's agenda in my life, your time is up. Die now, in Jesus' name.
5. You witchcraft strong man in my father's house that wants to make my life useless, die in Jesus'

name.

6. You ancient strong man in my family, holding the souls of men captive, I command you now, be dethroned, in the name of Jesus.
7. Let the wickedness of the wicked in my family come to an end, in the name of Jesus.
8. Strong man of my mother's linage, I command you to die by fire!
9. You wicked strong man working against the progress of sons and daughters from my village, expire by fire!
10. You wicked strong man assigned against my life, I invade your house with the anointing and fire of the Holy Ghost, I chain you, I destroy your weapons, and I release my goods in your custody, in the mighty name of Jesus.
11. Strong man assigned to waste, hinder or kill my destiny, die by fire, in the name of Jesus.
12. Every strong man frustrating and limiting my efforts, hindering my visions and dreams in life, by the blood of Jesus, I destroy your power!
13. Every strong man blocking or scattering my opportunities, I destroy your power and recover my lost opportunities, in the name of Jesus.
14. Every seed or point of contact of the strong man in me, used to monitor my investments and activities, receive fire, in Jesus' name.
15. All monitoring computers and satellite gadgets

of the strong man focused on me to trail me, I release the fire of God against you now, in the name of Jesus.

16. Every strong man assigned against my business, office and endeavours, die by fire, in the name of Jesus.
17. Every strong man assigned against my finances, be scattered, in the name of Jesus.
18. Every strong man assigned against my source of income, be scattered now, in the name of Jesus.
19. Every strong man assigned against my life to block my helpers and render me helpless, be scattered, in the name of Jesus.
20. Every strong man promoting destructive addictions and evil habits in my life, expire by fire, in the name of Jesus.
21. Strong man diverting my blessings, receive fire of destruction, in Jesus' name.
22. Strong man blocking my open gate of favour, lifting, success and breakthroughs, receive the stone of death, in Jesus' name.
23. In the precious name of Jesus, you strong man blocking the entrance to my new level of blessings, expire by fire!
24. Every strong man afflicting my body with sickness, take all your sicknesses out of my body now, in Jesus' name!
25. Every strong man sponsoring seasonal

sicknesses and afflictions in my life, die by fire, in the name of Jesus.

26. Strong man of infirmity tormenting my life; die by fire, in the name of Jesus.
27. Strong man of delay and stagnation frustrating my efforts, expire by fire, in the matchless name of Jesus.
28. Strong man in charge of poverty in my family; be destroyed by fire, in the mighty name of Jesus.
29. Strong man of hardship and struggle, die by fire, in the timeless name of Jesus.
30. Strong man assigned to destroy firstborns in my family, you are a liar, die by fire, in the mighty name of Jesus.
31. Strong man covering my marital, ministerial, financial, professional and academic star, expire by fire, in the mighty name of Jesus.
32. Strong man promoting evil patterns of divorce, adultery, single parenthood and late marriage in my bloodline, I destroy you, in Jesus' name.
33. Strong man promoting evil patterns of untimely death in my bloodline; receive judgment of death, in Jesus' name.
34. Strong man promoting evil patterns of failure at the edge of breakthrough, receive judgment of death, in Jesus' name.
35. Strong man in charge of evil patterns of failure, limitation, stagnation, delay and unfruitfulness

in my bloodline; be destroyed by fire, in Jesus' name.

36. Strong man hindering the arrival of my answered prayers, die by fire, in Jesus' name.
37. Oh God my Father, I decree, every strong man promoting evil patterns of struggle, hardship and poverty in my bloodline, expire by fire!
38. You strong man of business and financial losses; expire by fire, in the mighty name of Jesus.
39. Strong man working against my marital success, die by fire, in the mighty name of Jesus.
40. Strong man polluting my spiritual atmosphere with failure, rejection, and disappointment, die by fire!
41. You strong man that stopped my parents and you also want to stop me; I stop you and command you now to die, in the mighty name of Jesus.
42. Strong man assigned against my spiritual life, to weaken my prayer life, my understanding of the Word and block my spiritual sensitivity, die by fire, in the mighty name of Jesus.
43. Strong man assigned to my life from the day I was born, your time is up, die by fire, in Jesus' name.
44. Strong man assigned to manipulate my dream life with evil dreams and block me from remembering my dreams, scatter by fire, in

Jesus' name.

45. Strong man responsible for barrenness - lack of opportunities and waste of seasons in my life, today is your end, scatter by fire, in Jesus' mighty name.
46. Strong man in charge of pollution and desecration in my life, scatter by fire, in Jesus' mighty name.
47. Strong man assigned to abort my dreams and interrupt my process, die by fire, in Jesus' name.
48. Strong man responsible for terminating my evidence before I can enjoy it, receive fire of destruction, in the name of Jesus.
49. All my confiscated blessings in the strong man's house, I recover you, in Jesus' name.
50. All my confiscated opportunities in the strong man's house, I recover you and your accumulated arrears, in the mighty name of Jesus.

OTHER BOOKS BY
Bishop Abraham
CHIGBUNDU

- Voice of Freedom (Daily Devotional)
- Loose Him and Let Him Go
- I Believe in Deliverance
- Wicked Times and Seasons
- Witchcraft Manipulations Exposed
- Achievers Secrets
- Developing Another Spirit
- Discover to Recover
- Changing Wicked Times and Seasons'
- From Story to Glory
- Learning in the School of Marriage
- Altar versus Altars
- Spiritual Checkpoint
- Destined for Greatness but Tied
- 30 Secrets of Success
- How to Open Closed Human Destinies
- Overcoming Evil Waters
- Life Transforming Words of Bishop Abraham Chigbundu
- 7 Things God does not Know
- Abiding in His Presence

DR. ABRAHAM
CHIGBUNDU
BREAKING
FAULTY FAMILY
FOUNDATIONS

To Purchase Bishop Chigbundu's Books
visit www.amazon.com

TO PURCHASE **BISHOP CHIGBUNDU'S BOOKS**
VISIT WWW.AMAZON.COM

CHANGING
WICKED
TIMES & SEASONS
DR ABRAHAM
CHIGBUNDU

DESTINED
FOR
GREATNESS
But Tied
A Step-by-step Approach to Securing Your
Freedom, Untying Your Destiny, Breaking The
Cycle of Delay and Manifesting Greatness
DR ABRAHAM
CHIGBUNDU

www.ingramcontent.com/pod-product-compliance
Ingram Content Group UK Ltd.
Pitfield, Milton Keynes, MK11 3LW, UK
UKHW041638190726
13854UKWH00006B/2573

9 789785 764598